Blended Families Special Children

Blended Families Special Children

Build a Happy Stepfamily

Andrea Campbell

Pocket Learner Publishing

© Copyright Andrea Campbell 2021 - All rights reserved.

The content contained in this book may not be reproduced, duplicated or transmitted without direct written permission from the author or publisher. Under no circumstances will any blame or legal responsibility be held against the publisher, or author, for any damages, reparation, or monetary loss due to the information contained within this book; either directly or indirectly. You are responsible for your own choices, actions, and results.

Legal Notice:

This book is copyright protected and is only for personal use. You cannot amend, distribute, sell, use, quote or paraphrase any part, of this book without the consent of the author or publisher.

Disclaimer Notice:

Please note the information contained in this text is for educational and entertainment purposes only. All effort has been executed to present accurate, up-to-date, and reliable, complete information. No warranties of any kind are declared or implied. Readers acknowledge that the author is not engaging in the rendering of legal, financial, medical, or professional advice. The content within this book has been derived from various sources. Please consult a licensed professional before attempting any techniques outlined in this book.

By reading this document, the reader agrees that under no circumstances is the author responsible for any losses, direct or indirect, which are incurred as a result of the use of the information contained within this document, including, but not limited to - errors, omissions, or inaccuracies.

The inspirational quotes contained in these books are the intellectual property of Andrea Campbell. They may be referenced but always with attribution.

ISBN: 978-1-914997-29-7 (sc)   978-1-914997-30-3 (hc)

Table of Contents

Book 1 – Blended and Special

Introduction 1
Chapter 1 Launching 9
Chapter 2 Loving 35
Chapter 3 Listening 57
Chapter 4 Laughing 71
Chapter 5 Leading 89
Chapter 6 Letting 105
Chapter 7 Lifting 121
Chapter 8 Lubricating 133
Chapter 9 Learning 145
Conclusion 163
Resources 167

Book 2 - Blended Family

Preface 173
Introduction 177
Chapter 1 Bureaucracy 181
Chapter 2 Lambasting 187
Chapter 3 Unforgiveness 193
Chapter 4 Nepotism 199
Chapter 5 Dearth 205
Chapter 6 Ennui 213
Chapter 7 Reticence 219
Conclusion 225
Resources 233
Glossary 235

I would like to thank my family —

Richmond and Shari

for their inspiration, understanding and patience.

BLENDED AND SPECIAL

Nine Keys for Building a Happy Stepfamily Caring for a Child with Special Needs and Disabilities

for stepmoms and stepdads

Andrea Campbell

INTRODUCTION

A blended family comprises two parents, their children from previous relationships, and any child from their current union. It is more complicated than a traditional nuclear family, but it can also be more rewarding when you know how to function appropriately in a blended family. The thought of being in a blended family sounds uncomfortable for some of us. Still, many people who have been in an affectionate blended family will attest to the challenges and rewards of belonging to an unconventional family that loves you as their own. It is not the first choice of many to mingle intimately with people if they are not blood-related.

Complications may arise, and no one likes complicated relationships. You can expect bumps along the road if you decide to share the rest of your life with someone who has children from a previous relationship. When one or more of those children has a learning disability, the learning curve for a stepparent can be rather steep.

According to renowned family counselor Tom Frydenger: "Becoming a blended family means mixing, mingling, scrambling, and sometimes muddling our way through delicate family issues, complicated relationships, and individual differences, hurts, and fears. But through it all, we are learning to love like a family." That statement adequately encapsulates the experiences of blended families, which I've been a part of on both sides. I grew up in a blended family, and I am now a stepparent.

My parents separated when I was three years old, and my mother married and had four more children, one of whom had special educational needs. My stepfather's two children joined us, and we lived together as one big, blended family. Stepfamilies require additional levels of transition and acceptance depending on each partner's family history and personal circumstances. Flourishing in such a family involves considerable change. When one or more children have physical or intellectual disabilities, the process becomes complicated.

According to Science Daily, "In the United States and Canada, the term learning disability is used to refer to psychological and neurological conditions that affect a person's communicative capacities and potential to be taught effectively. Special education is the instruction that is provided to children who learn differently from their peers. The children may have physical disabilities, learning disabilities, developmental, behavioral or emotional disorders, or special gifts and talents. In the United Kingdom, the term learning disability is generally used to refer to developmental disability."

A learning disability manifests in a reduced intellectual ability and difficulty with everyday activities like self-care, household tasks, or money management. Some people may find it difficult to socialize or make and keep friends. They may also take longer to learn and find it difficult to understand complicated information. These characteristics usually affect a person throughout their life. They may need some level of long-term support, but many adults with a learning disability can lead independent lives with the appropriate support.

Learning disabilities are often confused with learning difficulties such as dyslexia or attention deficit hyperactivity disorder (ADHD). Autism is not a learning disability, but around half of the autistic people in the UK may also have a learning disability. It is sometimes referred to as a being on the spectrum or autism spectrum disorder (ASD). Dyslexia is a "learning difficulty" but not a learning disability, as it does not affect intellect.

I use the word "disability" in its loosest sense for this book to include those with intellectual disabilities or challenging behavior that someone with ADHD may display. The principles also apply where stepchildren have physical disabilities. There is no intent to be technical or scientific; instead, recognize that a learning difficulty or disability of any kind affects individuals differently. The material is also relevant to children who might not have been diagnosed with any disability but whose behavior is described as "challenging."

I will also occasionally use the word "special" when referring to a child with special needs and disabilities or a child with challenging behavior. It does not mean that other children are not special or that this child is more special. The focus of this text is to highlight how physical and cognitive impairments or challenges affect blended families and to share information on how stepfamilies can achieve a happy existence despite their daily challenges.

My daughter has Down syndrome. Her speech is severely delayed, but she has improved tremendously over the years based on the extensive work we have done with her at home. Some of her friends are diagnosed with developmental delay; others with autism and Asperger's syndrome. The range of known conditions is too vast to mention. Parents attracted to this book will know if any conditions apply to their child, and I hope that they will gain insight into how to maneuver through this unique field.

For example, someone on the autism spectrum may have rigid routines and struggle to connect interpersonally and emotionally. They may also have behavioral challenges that are new to the stepparent who, despite their best efforts, may not be equipped to cope with these attributes. It is no wonder, then, that many clinicians believe the divorce rate of blended families with autistic children to be higher than in the general population and in other stepfamilies.

There is reason for hope, though. In the study mentioned above, the researchers found that "Couples with neuro-typical children who can help care for and support their siblings with developmental disabilities may experience less marital stress. This phenomenon suggests that other children in the family may be a vital support system for parents coping with the care of a child with a developmental disability."

One of the biggest challenges to parents when their child is disabled can be accepting the child's disability. As expectant parents, we dream of what they will be like and what they will do as they grow up. However, when our child is born with a disability, those dreams are significantly altered, leaving you to rethink everything.

Laws in the United States (from the Individuals with Disabilities Education Act and the Elementary and Secondary Education Act) exist to protect the rights of children and adolescents ages 3–21 with special needs. These laws provide a bridge between early childhood and adulthood, continuity, enhanced communication, and a focus on family involvement and lifelong outcomes. Other than educational services, these laws may also provide additional support mechanisms such as transitional support, crisis management, and other appropriate services.

Many of the sentiments children in stepfamilies think, feel, and say are the same as children growing up in traditional families. In storybooks *we* read as children, the stepmom was always described as wicked and was the target of children's anger. When entering a stepfamily, children often blame the stepmom for replacing their biological parents. Most often, the stepmom or stepdad has nothing to do with the separation of the birth parents. Children with cognitive disabilities, many of whom cannot articulate their feelings verbally, may show their disapproval differently. Their behavior can baffle a new stepparent if they are unfamiliar with the child's diagnosis or not experienced in the field.

The key to raising happy stepchildren is effective communication. Parenting stepchildren can be challenging—you must be wise and sensitive, creative, and flexible in your approach to develop and maintain good relationships with your stepchildren. All children require patience, warmth, and compassion. Stepchildren and those with disabilities require these traits even more. From a very young age, they may be independent-thinking individuals with the potential to appear aggressive or rude. Any attempt to fight fire with fire will only stoke a massive blaze that can potentially burn your house down.

There are various reasons why the union of two parents and their kids from former relationships can prove challenging. For example, children might have had differing family routines and parenting styles. Conflicts surrounding visitation rights and tension between ex-partners may arise. Stepchildren may also have special needs, and the stepparent may lack experience related to the condition. As the early years of a blended family are more likely to be challenging, new stepparents often experience stress.

When a disabled child is part of the new stepfamily, it increases the dynamics in the home. If not understood before moving in, the stepparent may face a steep learning curve and throw the family off balance. Issues with stepchildren can cause stress in the relationship. Couples entering blended families with disabled children should recognize and accept that their world will change as they embrace new roles and build lasting relationships. While you as parents approach the concept of remarriage and the acquisition of a new family with immense excitement and expectation, your children or your new spouse's children might not share that sentiment.

For the most part, children will feel dubious and unsettled with the impending changes. As a result, they are more likely to be concerned about sharing their space with new stepsiblings. Forming a functional and stable blended family can be complicated if children frequently experience complex emotions. For example, if a disabled child is loud, the noise may disturb the other children and result in the absence of friendships. No one entertains the idea of living with people whom they barely know or may even dislike. For this reason, children may resist the change, and this resistance will play out in their behaviors.

Entering a blended family can be a complicated undertaking. As a parent, you may become frustrated when your new family does not gel immediately. But don't be discouraged, for time is a great healer. Families will adjust and ultimately achieve happiness over time—no matter how complex or uneasy things initially appear. With mutual respect, open communication, a generous amount of patience, and love, you can establish a close connection with your new stepchildren and form a successful, loving, happy blended family. And despite the highs and lows that unavoidably surface when two families come together, your blended family has the potential to become solid and supportive for all its members.

Since I know what it's like to be a stepchild and stepparent, I'd like to help you achieve a happy and peaceful family home. I am sharing information that I wish someone had provided for my family when I was a child. All my siblings and stepsiblings got on well from the beginning. However, my mother and stepfather had differing forms of discipline, which brought undue stress into the family. Thankfully, I learned early what works and what doesn't and thus avoided the pitfalls and maintained a happy stepfamily.

I'm sharing my experience of successful stepparenting in a home with a child who has special educational needs and disabilities. I hope that by implementing these steps, you'll simplify your transition into a new family structure or improve your existing stepfamily. You'll discover in this book that, despite the challenges you can expect while caring for a disabled child, it is possible to achieve the goal of creating a healthy and loving stepfamily with a fulfilling and harmonious life.

This book is structured around 9 Ls: Launching, Loving, Listening, Laughing, Leading, Letting, Lifting, Lubricating, and Learning. Together they provide valuable tips and techniques for raising a stepchild with a cognitive or physical disability. I know that your ultimate desire is to achieve a happy, successful stepfamily (with or without neurotypical children). You'll discover how to bond with your disabled stepchild, address your differences, strengthen your family, and maintain a happy relationship with your spouse so all the children in your family unit can feel safe and content.

Each chapter commences with one of my personal inspirational quotes. These words are my intellectual property and are included in the text to motivate you on your journey to becoming the best stepparent that money can't buy. Enjoy and be inspired!

This book will provide you with a good understanding of the joys and challenges that can come from being part of a blended family. It will help you and your partner ensure that your stepfamily is successful. The ability to positively impact the life of a child who is not yours biologically is a hugely rewarding experience when you get it right.

Chapter 1

LAUNCHING

"Plan your journey, even if you don't have a ride"

Getting accustomed to living in a stepfamily or blended family takes time. Studies reveal that, on average, it takes approximately two years to familiarize yourself with new family members and establish bonds. During this period, you and your partner will learn to work together to care for your children. You'll discover that it's a learning process and that you will not immediately have all the answers. Keep in mind that relationships take time. Every new member of your family will have to adjust at their own pace.

Following those crucial two years of bonding, families commonly get accustomed to new routines and daily life. Still, issues arise in all types of families, and blended families have countless unique challenges that many people do not recognize until they are in the situation. Understanding what to expect in a blended family can help stepparents manage conflicts before they escalate.

Managing Expectations

Family therapists revealed that creating a healthy stepfamily is a daunting task. The process can take anywhere from two to seven years with significant adjustments. Attempting to combine two families too quickly might lead to frustration since some family members might resist bonding. Therefore, it is imperative to first work on the couple's relationship. That's the primary step to creating a healthy and happy blended family. It is essential to spend quality time with your partner and take care of each other through open and positive communication.

Nurturing your relationship is particularly valuable because the bonds you and your partner have with your biological children began way before (and might be more solid than) your relationship with your spouse. Relationships can be hard work, and no two are the same. Part of that hard work involves dealing with pain, loss, and anguish from a previous marriage or relationship. Guilt, loss, and rejection from an earlier marriage or relationship can manifest in ways neither partner understands or expects. When you combine those factors with caring for a disabled child, the issues increase exponentially.

Honesty is the best policy in blended families (and really, in all families). You'd be surprised how much honesty in your relationship can save your marriage and family. There is no point in concealing the severity of your child's disability from your partner while you're dating. If you are sincere and honest from the beginning, you give your partner a chance to make an informed decision about advancing the relationship. You may lose your connection if they decide that the situation would be too much to handle. If that's the case, it's best to be upfront and honest early on.

With sincerity and open communication, you and your spouse will be well on your way to building a solid foundation. When challenges arise, make a concerted effort to work with your partner to find solutions. If the disabled child is your biological child, you will want to support the child, but always remember that you and your partner are a team—the rock upon which the family is built. It is no easy task to manage these dynamics when choosing between your spouse and child. For these reasons, you must ensure that your partner is exposed to your child's issues—tantrums, demands, and other peculiarities—before entering into marriage or a permanent relationship. No two days will be the same. There will be moments when new behaviors emerge, and you must ensure that you have done your best to prepare your partner for those moments.

You must present a united front in the presence of all your children, even if you feel they lack the cognitive ability to comprehend discord. Don't make the mistake of underestimating how much your child understands or doubting their ability to manipulate situations. For instance, if you disagree with how your spouse handles a specific problem, discuss your concerns privately in a non-judgmental manner and not in the presence of children.

You have likely learned through experience that establishing a healthy relationship does not happen overnight. It requires commitment, effort, time, and patience. As a new couple with kids from a previous marriage or relationship, you can expect to encounter unique challenges. When your new family includes a child with special needs, those challenges will be compounded, and everyone will need to adjust the expectations for their new family unit. The learning curve may be steep for the stepparent and their children, increasing frustration as routines change to accommodate the disabled child.

Family issues arise in all families, but blended families have unique challenges that many parents do not realize until they enter a new relationship. Those issues multiply when the family unit cares for a child with special needs, especially when the stepparent is unprepared for this new role.

Children often feel apprehensive, anxious, or uneasy toward new stepparents. It is usually easier for them to bond with stepsiblings. When a child has a disability, additional learning and adjustments are required. Challenges can be alleviated if everyone in your blended family knows each other before embarking on a life together. And while it is okay for kids to feel uneasy, it is necessary to establish ground rules making it clear that hostile behavior toward family is unacceptable. Your children must understand that they need to treat your new partner or spouse with respect and kindness.

You, as a stepparent, must also be respectful to the children—respect is a two-way street. You should avoid having the exact expectations for your blended family that you had for a previous family arrangement. Do not expect to superimpose your biological family into your blended family and continue as usual (even if you think your stepchildren are culturally similar to your biological children).

As you and your new partner work to build your new household, share with them your previous household rules, discipline styles, and responsibilities. Understanding these rules will help your partner support you to make responsibilities and rules coherent for your biological children. Your spouse needs to give you the same information regarding your stepchildren. You must acknowledge that you have a bond with your child that your new partner does not share as a birth parent (and vice-versa). This bond is crucial in the case of disabled children. Include your partner in your daily routines related to caring for a child with special needs as much as possible. Be sensitive, and understand that your partner may feel apprehensive if they lack information about the condition and caring regimens for a child with those particular needs.

Considerations before Moving in Together

Individuals planning a life together with children from former partners must remember that the children had lives before with another parent. Before moving in together, partners must consider a range of factors to improve the possibility of achieving a happy stepfamily.

Essential Details about Moving In

Jot down a range of positive and negative emotions. You can do this on your own, or you can share it with your partner. Consider your feelings about moving in and that of the children involved. Are you happy, nervous, excited, anxious, relieved, or still mourning and having regrets about the past? When you do this with children, you must prepare for varying opinions. While children might agree on the nervousness and excitement, they might express agonies and resentments from the past.

Children are generally more sensitive and might feel hurt at the idea that their old family is gone. Without fail, the most excellent way of dealing with discomfort and sad feelings is by bringing them out into the open and tackling all issues head-on. Ensure that your children get time and space to talk without reprimanding them for saying how they truly feel.

Some children display unpleasant behavior, refuse to communicate, or isolate themselves due to unhappy emotions. Reassure and encourage them. Be honest and avoid imposing sanctions for negative behaviors they may demonstrate during this uncertain time. Clearing up such issues will give the children the security they require during the transition phase. During the process of moving in, ask your children what they like, dislike, and how they feel.

Everyone needs to know about the new move, too. Consider all the potential dynamics—will children be living with you full-time or part-time? Are you moving to a new house, or is one partner moving in with their children? (Kindly note that this is even more significant when there are two sets of children involved.)

Sharing Space Positively

Children joining a blended family will require a space they can call their own. They need to feel they have a place even if they visit infrequently. If they have a room for themselves, ensure that space will be exclusively for them, and their privacy will be assured. Or, if they need to share a room, establish the dynamics early. Sharing a room with a child with learning difficulties may not be an easy option and should be avoided if possible.

While you would like the children to get along, it is unfair and unwise to force the neurotypical children to endure non-typical behavior if they find it annoying. It is critical to include all members of the family in the plans. Discuss relevant issues like respect for each other's personal property and privacy. Also, teach the principles to your special child but bear in mind they may break the rules depending on their level of cognitive awareness.

Creating Plans to Live Together

Moving in can take place gradually or in stages. For example, one of you might stay the night and leave the following day. Then you may spend the weekends, or perhaps a few days until finally, you both decide that it is time to combine families and share a home. It may be the home of one of the stepparents, or you might find a new place. I understand the concerns about moving into the house of one stepparent—this can cause your children anxiety. I recall my mother moving into my stepfather's house and the transition progressing smoothly. It is not always possible to find a new place, so work within your circumstances. If your child has a physical disability, you may need to consider the configuration of the new home. You may need to avoid high-rise buildings with or without elevators.

If you successfully implement the initial preparations—i.e., if the children get to know each other beforehand and if opportunities are created for them to carry out activities together—the moving-in process can be smooth.

As your moving-in date approaches, it might feel like a typical day for you and your partner since shared living has somehow become a routine. However, this isn't always the case for children. It is essential to ascertain how the children feel before your new spouse or partner moves in. This will make it easier to address and resolve issues.

Managing the "Moving In" Day

Moving can cause stress and stimulate mixed emotions. But it can be managed so long as you allow everyone to take part in the process. Ask your new partner and stepchildren for some ideas on how they want to transform the rooms and other areas of the house. Consider redecorating the place. Be flexible and recognize that room allocation might not remain the same for an extended time. You also need to consider that the children are growing.

Financial Issues

Managing finance as a couple can be challenging enough. Things can get more complicated in a second marriage or relationship, with or without children. Financial matters in a blended family are not typically straightforward, but you can iron them out with proper discussion, planning, and management.

Money is generally an uncomfortable topic. But being honest upfront about how you think and feel is necessary. This will allow you to inhibit any discomfort, quarrels, and significant financial issues in the future. Things can get tricky when you decide to be in a blended family because it is not only about you and your new spouse. It is also about your stepchildren and extended family members. Children with disabilities attract additional expenses for items like travel (they may need a particular vehicle or a carrier), therapies, medicines, and special diets.

Financial planning is always a necessary element of family life, but if you create a blended family with a disabled child, you must carefully plan your finances. The finances checklist for blended families below will assist you in starting the financial conversations you need to have. Here are five subjects that stepparents should address when developing financial plans and saving goals:

1. *Living arrangements* - Are you going to purchase or rent a place? Decide if you will reside in a house that was once shared with an ex-partner or spouse. Is there adequate space for your special child to have their own space? Is there appropriate access to the room with or without the need for an elevator?

2. *Estate planning and life insurance* - These refer to asset protection. Life insurance offers wealth-protecting benefits by providing a way to transfer wealth to your beneficiaries and helping provide funds to pay estate taxes. Based on a family's needs and situation, an estate planning lawyer can assist in selecting and executing strategies that work best.

3. *Spousal support obligations* - Check out how long and how much your spouse will support their absent children or ex-spouse. Read your partner's parenting agreement and divorce decree to learn more about their obligations.

4. *Paying for children's education* - You might want to learn about your partner's financial obligation for college. Generally, this divides between the biological parents as per their income. Your disabled child may need to attend a specialist school. In the absence of publicly funded transportation, you will need to cover

the extra costs of attending said school. Typically, your neurotypical children will be able to travel to school once they are old enough. However, this procedure may not work for your special child.

5. *Vacation plans* - Be specific about the frequency of going on vacation as a couple and with other extended family members. Set a budget for the expenses covering the entire vacation. Don't forget to factor in the needs of your special child. Some destinations may be out of bounds as some children may find air travel particularly challenging.

Discussing how you want to spend and save money now that you are a blended family is crucial to financial success. Finance is a topic of conversation that can cause ceaseless arguments, mental suffering, and conflict. Think and work as a team with a shared vision and goals for the future. Financial disagreements can negatively impact even a solid relationship or one where money is not an issue. If necessary, seek expert financial advice to address financial difficulties.

Differences emerge when you combine families. One way to lessen the conflict and tension is to address money matters sooner rather than later. Open and honest discussions about your combined finances can lead to better management of money and ensure that there is enough to support the needs and lifestyle of every member of the stepfamily. When thinking about how to manage your finances as a blended family, it helps to:

- Ensure that resources, assets, and budgets are fair for all children.

- Discuss and weigh the options and make decisions before moving in together.
- Consider what each of you could contribute to house repairs or mortgages.
- Maintain an open conversation as new considerations emerge (for example, the financial implications of welcoming a new baby).
- Keep an eye on legal agreements for finances in matters such as loans and liens.

Case Study of a Special Child

> *Children with special educational needs display a range of behaviors that may prove challenging to new stepparents. The attitudes vary widely. Your new stepchild may demonstrate one, several, or none of them. The short story of Jack below brings out some of these behaviors. It is not meant to shock you but rather prepare you for the worst-case scenario as you attempt to build a happy stepfamily caring for a child with special needs or challenging behavior.*
>
> *Jack is a nine-year-old pupil in an elementary school. This morning, Jack's dad had to use a different route to take Jack to school because the local authority was laying a new road surface. And because the road was closed, Jack was late for school.*
>
> *Jack hates being late. He hates to walk into class when all the other children are milling about. So, he waits in the cloakroom until they've all gone in. Mrs. Brown said it was okay for him to do that.*

When Max steps into class, Mrs. Brown isn't there. Instead, a stranger is standing at the front with the Principal. Mrs. Brown has gone on a course today, and they have a substitute teacher named Mrs. Green. But Jack doesn't know this because he came in late. So, he sits down when the Principal tells him to and wonders when Mrs. Brown will arrive.

Mrs. Green announces that the class spelling test will be first. Jack has been trying hard with his spelling and has practiced at home. Mrs. Green starts to read the words out, but they're not in the correct order. Jack feels a knot in his stomach and writes out the spelling test he has learned in the appropriate order. He scores two out of ten, and the teacher tells him that he will have to try harder. Jack likes stickers, but he didn't get a smiley face as usual.

At break time, Jack goes out into the playground. He's got an apple for a snack. As he eats it, a girl bumps into him, and it drops on the floor. One of the boys kicks it across the playground, and it ends up in a puddle. Jack goes to get it and gets his feet wet. He hates being wet, so he goes back into class and takes his shoes and socks off.

Mrs. Green almost trips over Jack's feet as he is sitting right in the classroom doorway. She tells Jack to put his sneakers on. He responds that it is not time for P.E. yet, so he can't put on his sneakers.

Mrs. Green glares at Jack and suggests that he might prefer to sit outside the Principal's office. Jack is quite happy with this suggestion; it's nice and quiet in the corridor. He puts his sneakers on, but they don't feel right without socks, and all he can think about is how itchy they are on his feet.

On the way out of the classroom, he sees the girl that bumped into him in the playground. He pushes her back, and then she tells the teacher that he pushed her for no reason. So, Mrs. Green walks over to Jack. She's wearing strong perfume, and he wants to wretch. When she asks him why he is making faces, he says it's because she smells.

Mrs. Green marches Jack down the corridor and tells the Principal that Jack is naughty and very rude. Jack tells her she is lying. The Principal tells Jack to sit there until he feels he can behave. It suddenly starts to rain heavily. The Principal remarks that it is raining cats and dogs, which baffles Jack as he could not see any cats or dogs.

After half an hour outside the Principal's office, Jack feels much calmer, so he decides to return to his classroom. Still no Mrs. Brown. When the bell goes for lunch, Jack puts his hands over his ears and runs to the classroom door to be first. Mrs. Green tells him off for pushing and makes him wait at the end of the queue. When he goes to get his lunchbox, he can't find it; it's not where he left it with his coat.

When the Teaching Assistant manages to calm him down, she arranges to have a school lunch instead. He has to sit at a different table in the hall, and the smell of other people's lunches makes him feel ill. He looks down and notices that the beans are touching the potatoes, so he can't eat that now. Dry food shouldn't touch wet foods. Everyone is talking, and the noise of cutlery and scraping of chairs is overwhelming.

Jack goes back to the classroom and lies on the floor with his coat over his head. The ground is nice and cool, and he starts to feel regulated. However, he makes the Teaching Assistant jump when she walks past him. She chastises him, saying, "You scared me to death, Jack!"

Jack is concerned about this because he likes her and doesn't want her to die. But, she carries on walking as though she is okay. So, he follows her to the playground, just to make sure.

After lunch, Mrs. Green tells the class to get into pairs. Jack sits at a table with two other children who have already paired up. He doesn't know what to do. Finally, Mrs. Green asks for anyone who's not sitting with someone to put up their hand. Jack doesn't realize she's talking to him—he's sitting with two people, so he doesn't put his hand up; after all, he is not sitting alone. When Mrs. Green raises her voice and asks why he wasn't paying attention, it all becomes a bit of a blur, and Jack has no idea why he is being told off again. He wonders if it is because he made the Teaching Assistant die. He really can't remember what happens after that.

The bell goes at the end of the day, and Jack goes out to find his Stepmom.

"Did you have a good day at school, Jack?" asks his Stepmom.

> *Instead of responding, Jack decides to lay down in the street; he'd come to the end of his road and could no longer hold it in.*
>
> *(Think of Jack as a bottle of soda pop. As he goes through the day, the bottle gets shaken each time there is a trigger, with the pressure building up as his stress and anxiety increase. Jack managed to hold it all together while at school, but when his Stepmom picked him up, he had a meltdown—the pop was released from the bottle in one go. Many stepparents experience the Pop Effect—the delayed meltdown, which follows a day of triggers and masking.)*
>
> *Jack arrives home and locks himself in his room. The door does not have a lock, but Jack sits behind the door. When he emerges twenty minutes later, he has wet himself. He has also battered and bruised his face. His stepmom is the first person he sees, and she attempts to hug him. Jack shouts in her face, and without warning, he hits her in her stomach. She retreats. Jack's stepsister, Trudy, is scared of Jack when he gets into this mode, so she runs to her room and cries. Dad walks in, and finally, Jack calms down. Although Jack has no issues with speech, he refuses to talk for the rest of the evening.*

The preceding story exemplifies challenges a stepparent may face when the stepfamily unit includes a special child. This is not meant to scare you but rather to prepare you for your unique journey, which, like any other family, will have its ups and downs. The range of behaviors you may encounter is wide-ranging. But whatever the situation, if you follow the suggestions in this book, you will be well on your way to coping and thriving as a stepparent.

State Benefits for Which You May be Eligible

Stepparents should be aware that the parents, caregivers, or representatives of children younger than age 18 who have disabilities might make them eligible for Supplemental Security Income (SSI) payments. According to the United States Social Security Administration, SSI makes monthly payments to people with limited income and resources 65 or older, blind, or disabled. If younger than age 18, your child can qualify if they have a medical condition or combination of conditions that meets Social Security's definition of disability for children and if their income and resources fall within the eligibility limits.

The amount of the SSI payment is different from state to state because some states add to the SSI payment. Your local Social Security office can provide more information about this payment and how to apply. Be prepared to present detailed information about your child's medical condition and how it affects their ability to perform daily activities. You will also be asked to permit the doctors, teachers, therapists, and other professionals who have information about your child's condition.

The support is also for adults who became disabled in childhood (before age 22), and who might be entitled to Social Security Disability Insurance (SSDI) benefits. There are also employment support programs for young people with disabilities who are able and want to go to work.

When your child gets SSI, you'll be referred to places where you can access health care services for them. These services are under the Children with Special Health Care Needs provision of the Social Security Act. Medicaid is a health care program for people with limited income and resources. In most states, children who get SSI payments qualify for Medicaid. In many States, Medicaid comes automatically with SSI eligibility. In other states, you must sign up for it. Some children can get Medicaid coverage even if they don't qualify for SSI. Check with your state Medicaid agency or your state or county social services office for more information.

Medicare is a federal health insurance program that you may also be able to access. The Social Security Administration website www.ssa.gov provides additional information regarding these programs.

Cultural Differences

Why is it important to honor and talk through cultural, gender, and racial dynamics in blended families? First, if your new partner and their children have different backgrounds were raised differently, they must pay attention to these identities and talk them through. Second, it is essential to learn more about each other's identities before moving in together.

Avoid conventional thinking or using your background as a master guide. Such expectations could merely introduce more challenges to your blended family. It is imperative to acknowledge that you and your new partner are not replacing anyone but establishing further open communication and trusting relationships.

For instance, if your stepchildren are used to having a stay-at-home mother, they might require more guidance and attention from a parent when initially moving in. Understanding cultural and racial differences can significantly benefit bonding with your new partner and their kids. Finally, the adjustment that blended families (particularly the stepparents) often need to make could mean searching for a family physician, extracurricular instructors, afterschool coaches, or other groups that perfectly match their upbringing and background.

When it comes to different identities, there are instances when you or your new partner might not instantly become a child's confidant, especially with particular areas or concerns. Reaching a point of established trust isn't always easy. However, this dynamic does not need to weaken your relationship with your new partner and your kids. On the contrary—understanding these slight differences can help you promote stronger relationships and more respect for one another. It is fundamental to communicate openly and effectively when you are in a cross-cultural relationship. There are seven elements required for cross-cultural communication to be effective: respect, self-awareness, empathy, tolerance, humor, flexibility, and patience.

- *Respect* - Consider learning about your stepfamily's culture in specific ways. For example, you can ask questions, research their background, learn their language, and read. Aside from these, you can also try active listening. You will find that learning and understanding the differences between your, and your stepfamily's culture can result in well-improved cross-cultural communication and increased respect for one another.

- *Self-awareness* - It is vital to know yourself well and have a deeper understanding of your reaction to differences. Your values and knowledge of the world significantly affect your perception of what other people are saying and doing. To understand your stepfamily and other people, you've got to know and understand yourself first. For example, if you have never cared for a disabled child, you may not know how you feel about that experience. There is a saying, "circumstances make people," so chances are you will adapt to the situation. Still, this by no means guarantees that you will embrace your new role.

- *Empathy* - To give you a newer and better impression of the world and the people around you, you must appreciate how others feel. This acknowledgment is vital for cross-cultural communication. To understand others better, try to put yourself in their shoes.

- *Tolerance* - You need to recognize that people's behavior can be unclear or have more than one meaning. Someone's culture or background often dictates their social behavior and language. You can improve your cross-cultural communications if you remain open-minded or receptive to behavior that might vary in meaning based on the culture of the individual.

- *Humor* - Laughter is an essential ingredient in the cross-cultural stepfamily. Without humor, you're more likely to lose your perspective and sense of humanity. Rather than taking things too personally, try to laugh when there is miscommunication. Be mindful, however, of the limits. Realize when to crack a joke and when to be serious.

- *Flexibility* - Flexibility is essential for dealing with new and challenging situations. These moments require optimum emotional intelligence in the form of self-awareness. You should be able to handle outcomes effectively when they veer off-course, and you can salvage a situation so that it does not imperil your fundamental values.

- *Patience* - Living in a cross-cultural stepfamily and communicating cross-culturally can be challenging. Always remind yourself that growth and improvement in your new family take time. Make a concerted effort to practice patience. Remember that patience is a virtue.

Relationships with Birth Families

Your stepchildren will probably have deep relationships with their birth families. And now that they will be part of your stepfamily, it does not mean they will no longer yearn for their birth family. You must be prepared to facilitate visits and other forms of meetups so that your stepchildren can continue to sustain pre-established meaningful relationships.

Extended Family Relationships

Relationships with other family members such as grandparents, uncles, aunts, and cousins usually change after the death of a parent, divorce, and separation. So, it's more likely that you'll lose touch with your previous spouse's family. Or you may keep in touch, but it will naturally and gradually minimize in the long run. If you have a new partner or you remarried, you can expect more changes.

You will gain new in-laws, and your children will meet new grandparents, family members, and extended family. Children can typically take advantage of the connection with extended family members, provided that the connections are healthy and positive.

It is natural for children to like the feeling of belonging and to have plenty of people who love and look after them. Grandparents often play vital roles in looking after, teaching, and encouraging kids during their parents' entry into a new relationship, separation, remarriage, or when one parent passes away.

Sustaining Current Extended Family Relationships

There are moments, holidays, and special occasions that you share with your new partner that will require flexibility. For instance, stepchildren must have the opportunity to visit their other relatives. You may need to share your stepchildren with other relatives during special occasions, holidays, Thanksgiving Day, and other gatherings. If your child has learning difficulties, you will need to document step-by-step information and instructions regarding the care of your child. If your child has physical disabilities and has a wheelchair or other mobility equipment, consider whether you will need a particular type of vehicle to transport this equipment.

Many families perceive it as less complicated when the mother or father gets in touch with their extended families. Therefore, when kids live with either parent, they should be allowed contact with the other parent's extended family. Some families gather during special occasions such as weddings, graduations, holidays, birthdays, and other celebrations. Such special events generally go well when both families cooperate. But suppose your ex-partner lives far away, is estranged from family, does not keep in touch, or has died. In that case, the extent of the relationships with your children's relatives will rely primarily on your circumstances and decisions.

You may want to consider whether your previous partner's parents and other family members are important to your child and whether they wish to see and meet them. If your child is happy to see or meet them, and if your previous partner does not have a problem keeping the connection with them, then all is well.

Cultivating Relationships

The moment you remarry or enter a new relationship, your children will perhaps get new step-grandparents. Some step-grandparents are more enthusiastic about being involved compared to other family members. Some of these extended family members might find the presence of a disabled child in the family to be daunting. This attitude may be due to their inexperience or ignorance of the condition. Some people may be scared for the family; it is your duty to educate them and quell their fears.

If all family members are okay with it, children can cultivate supportive, friendly, and intimate connections with step-grandparents and other relatives.

How intimate this bond becomes could rely on the following:

- The interest and ability of step-grandparents and other relatives to connect with your child
- The age of your child when he meets the step-grandparents and other relatives. (Generally, young children develop closeness more quickly)

- How welcoming you and your children are in learning more about your relatives and step-grandparents.
- How well your step-grandparents and relatives cope with your child's disability.
- The amount of quality time that your child spends with relatives and step-grandparents.

You can fully encourage your children to cultivate bonds with step-grandparents and other relatives by attending special gatherings where you're invited. You may also consider organizing special events with your new extended family members if you don't feel any discomfort in doing so. This strategy may be preferable in the early stages, especially if your child displays particularly challenging behavior. Some parents of autistic children find it extremely stressful if their child kicks off outside the home. Consequently, they avoid or minimize these encounters. Each stepfamily will have to decide when and where to take their special child.

Also, if your child has physical disabilities, you must first check to see if there is appropriate access to the venue. You don't want to arrive at an address only to find that you have to get to the 10th floor and the elevator is out of service. I'd encourage you to find creative ways of enriching your special child's life experience. It is not fair or healthy to keep them away from other people for extended periods.

Overall, chapter 1 asserts that creating a blended family is an excellent opportunity to strengthen your love for your new partner. However, challenges and conflicts could adversely impact the relationship. When a child with special needs is part of a blended family, there are additional factors to consider. For these reasons, you must acknowledge the importance of planning and preparation, and endeavor to address any concerns early on in the relationship.

A Short Anecdote

Dianne is a stepdaughter who found herself at the other end of the spectrum in more ways than one. At 19, she became a stepmother herself. According to Dianne, her stepmother entered her life when she was very young. The only memory she has of a family was the blended one when her stepmother married her father. She had always looked up to her stepmother, but never in her wildest dreams had she imagined that she would become one herself. But she was ready to take on the challenge. After all, she had experienced it, and she understood it—or so she thought.

When she met her partner, they thought it would be easy for them. They had false hopes in thinking it would be a walk in the park. She thought she had it under control. But each blended family is different. False hopes can get you in trouble. As Dianne integrated herself into her husband Sam's family, she knew she'd entered a different world.

Just like her stepmother, Dianne became a stepmother to a young daughter. Sam's daughter was only four years old and had recently been diagnosed with autism. And at 19, Dianne was uncertain of her ability to care for this young non-verbal child who was already displaying challenging behavior.

Dianne also had difficulties with Sam's ex, but she stuck it out just like her stepmother had. Stepping into her stepmother's shoes was not easy, but in time, Dianne characterized it as the best and most rewarding choice she had ever made. Being a part of her stepdaughter's formative years has been a blessing for her. Not only has she honored her stepmother by being one herself, but she has also touched a little child's life. Now, she could never be prouder and happier with the journey she chose.

Whether you are new to blended families or not, challenges will emerge. You have to work hard if you want to live in a happy stepfamily unit.

Chapter 2

LOVING

"Love says yes and love says no, love holds on and love lets go; love is being and love is doing; love is really understanding"

Love is the ultimate universal language. It is a stepparent's role primarily to establish a substantial and loving foundation in a blended family. A family built on love will boast an unshakable foundation that will weather the inevitable storms of life. Conflict, jealousy, stress, and anxiety are all factors that plague stepfamilies. When love becomes your highest goal, you will create a healthy environment conducive to building solid, life-lasting relationships. In this chapter, I will share with you the factors involved in ensuring that love is the bedrock of your stepfamily.

A Foundation of Love

Love is a word that people tend to use loosely, but let's face it — it's not an automatic sentiment or action. Genuine love needs time to grow. You cannot force it; you must nurture it. Becoming a stepparent is a lifelong commitment, so do not take this decision lightly and be prepared to work on your relationship continuously. Children with special needs present more challenges but can also evoke the most rewarding emotions when you get it right. If you want a peaceful life, you must make a concerted effort to love your stepchildren as your own, irrespective of any disabilities and associated behaviors they may portray. Recognize that their disability is part of who they are. It is what makes them unique. The ensuing paragraphs reveal various ways to build a solid foundation of love for your blended family.

Nurture and Protect the Relationship with your Partner

If you are to have a successful stepfamily, you first need to become a successful couple. The longevity and happiness of the whole family will depend on the quality and strength of your relationship. A solid marital bond is crucial to the success of your stepfamily.

Parents usually feel considerable loyalty to their children since they've developed long-lasting bonds with them. However, partners need to present a united front to the kids in their homes. Regardless of a child's age or disability, they can recognize when parents are not on good terms. They can grasp the opportunity to play one parent against the other. This behavior is not unique to blended families with disabled children, but it can be more detrimental.

To maintain a happy home, partners should be open and honest with each other. Communication is vital in any successful relationship. Both of you must convey your feelings to each other clearly. It must also be the same message that you express to your children. If there is a change of mind, talk to your partner before relaying it to the kids—you don't want to send mixed messages.

There are times when your opinions do not match and may even conflict with your values. Without thinking, you may become defensive because your partner is so far out of sync with your way of thinking. If that happens, pull yourself back, gather your thoughts, then respond. Try to avoid conflict by listening and negotiating. (There is more about this in Chapter 3 on Listening.)

Another way to nurture your relationship is to spend time together as a couple. That means you may need to schedule a time to enjoy each other's company and focus on each other rather than the children. Caring for a disabled child takes more planning and may cost money for caregivers if the family is unavailable to cover. In some cases, siblings may assist, but keep in mind that minors are children and should not have caring responsibilities while left on their own. When choosing your options, ensure you operate within the law governing the age children may be left alone.

Take a short break, visit a museum, or enjoy some other activity that you both enjoy. We continue to grow and change throughout our lives, and taking time to keep in touch with your partner will prevent you from growing apart. Life in contemporary society is fast and demanding. We are constantly chasing money and paying bills. Qualitative actions like spending time together are sometimes neglected, and our families suffer as a result. We *must* have conversations on a range of subjects, including our fears, anxieties, hopes, dreams, and the factors in our community and society that affect us as a family.

Activities for the Whole Family

Doing activities together solidifies family relationships. They help family members get to know each other deeper. Some family activities that blended families might enjoy include: playing games, camping, hiking, swimming, renovating the house, vacations, going on long car rides, and many more.

All these activities allow you to spend more quality time together and create memories worth remembering. By including the entire family in planning the activities, everyone feels more dedicated and involved. You must ensure that your special child is informed about the plans, even if you think they cannot fully understand what is about to happen. Treat your child as what he is: a child. Involve him and let him play his part in preparations. Never assume he is not interested or cannot play a role in family activities.

Establish New Traditions

Without fail, family traditions build feelings of unity and teamwork. They help families establish a sense of identity. Stepfamilies can take advantage of this since members need to make an effort to feel like a typical family.

Special occasions such as Christmas, Thanksgiving, and New Year can be perfect opportunities to create new traditions. You can prepare new menus, but you also need to try cooking the preferred recipe of each family member.

Meanwhile, if they are used to sharing the occasions with extended family, you may allow them to do so; however, consider consolidating new activities to set a good balance between change and stability.

Spend Time in one-on-one Relationships

While it is true that spending time together as a family is favorable and indispensable, members should also reach out to one another one-on-one. Children often feel off-put by a new spouse or stepsibling. It is essential to allow them to have private time with their biological parent to reassure them that they are significant.

Stepparents must also spend private time with their stepchildren. For example, they could go shopping together, go to a hair salon, go for a walk, or watch a movie together. The activity will depend on the age and interests of the child. It will also depend on the level of cognitive ability of the child. If the child is challenged behaviorally, you will need to use strategies for coping with these behaviors while the child is in public.

Do not be tempted to take the easy way out by avoiding opportunities to take the child out in public. Do not hide your child from the world. They are a part of the world and have a unique role to play. Give them a chance to see the world and mix with people outside the home, however difficult it may be. One-to-one activities can establish an adult/child bond and banish any discomfort or awkwardness as you get to know each other.

It is also good practice to encourage activities amongst stepsiblings. This action should not be confused with older stepsiblings looking after a younger or disabled sibling. The time we are talking about here is *leisure* time. It works better when the ages are not too far apart, and there is no suggestion of one caring for the other. When people have fun together, the chances of developing lasting friendships are enhanced. This is a highly advantageous situation to a blended family. While it may take more time and present a higher level of intricacy, neurotypical step-siblings and those children diagnosed with physical and cognitive disabilities can also form solid friendships and bonds.

An Attitude of Acceptance

Parenting someone else's children is truly one of the most demanding roles. But it can also be one of the most fulfilling when you get it right. For this to happen, you must be ready, mentally and physically, to cope with the responsibility. It will test your patience, and on some days, you may regret taking on the role. But if your relationship with your partner is strong, you will weather the storm together. And if you have children of your own, you'll have some parenting experience which will come in handy.

There are many nuances to stepparenting that aren't obvious when caring for your biological children. Stepchildren come with behaviors, routines, and expectations that may be foreign to you. Sometimes there may be a steep learning curve as you navigate your way through this new way of life.

When you assume an attitude of accepting your stepchildren as they are, you will be better able to handle any resentment that may come your way. You will understand that their hostility towards you is a result of the turmoil in their lives.

Children crave stability. In most cases, their troubles will have nothing to do with you, but it is you who they see. Children with cognitive disabilities may be confused by the change of scene. They may not have the capacity to appreciate why things are changing, and they may be missing the stability they enjoyed having both of their parents under one roof.

When you start dating their biological parent, you do so with the understanding that their children are their responsibility, and they may need to live with you. You agree to accept them as they are, and you care for them with love despite the emotional baggage they may carry. It is disconcerting when they disrespect you, for you know the effort you are putting into helping to raise them. But they are children, and you must take the high road and display empathy. It's possible they've been through many emotional and physical disturbances and are simply not handling it well.

Your stepchildren may initially regard you as an intruder and even blame you for the breakup of their family. They might also be subject to outside influences from their biological family and may be confused by the various messages from different parties. These circumstances explain why you need a strong relationship with your partner, as you will need to fall back on their communication and support to help you. If you are the subject of abuse, you must speak up. Do not allow yourself to be trampled, and make every effort to protect your mental and physical health.

As a stepparent of a child with special needs, the possibility of abuse is real. In those cases, you must not take it personally. Focus on understanding the disability and finding help from medical personnel, professionals in the field, and parents of children with similar issues. Depending on the nature and level of the disability, you may even find yourself suffering physical abuse. Some children are a danger to themselves and others. You need to understand that the child is not usually hurting you because they are evil. They have a condition, and their behavior is a manifestation of that condition.

I have had first-hand experiences being kicked and head-butted by a child with ADHD visiting us with his mother. She is a single mother who describes her life as a living nightmare. She indicated that all her relationships had failed because none of her suitors wanted to take on her son. If your stepfamily includes a child with these behaviors, you should consider attending training programs to learn how to parent these children. You will need to learn how to restrain the child safely and discover what therapies could help. You also may need to seek assistance from the health authorities to ascertain whether the child has an invisible medical condition that is causing their challenging behavior. Many diseases are hidden; it is good practice to rule out the possibilities of their existence rather than introduce sanctions.

The following are some methods for creating a more solidified blended family while simultaneously caring for a disabled child:

- *Love* - It is crucial to provide children with adequate attention. Show them that they are loved every day. This love may take the form of cuddles, praise, or the utterance of reassuring statements like "I love you." Children with special needs generally require these gestures more than neurotypical children.

- *Honest and open communication* - It is best to give your kids unwavering attention as often as possible. Urge them to talk openly about their feelings. Assure them that they can tell you anything because you are more than willing to listen to them. If your child uses sign language, try to learn the signs and encourage other family members to do so.

- *Positive reinforcement* - Encourage and applaud your children more often. Make them feel cherished and appreciated. Recognize the efforts of your special child and come up with unique ways of making them feel valued.

- *Respect* - You can't force all members of your stepfamily to like each other. However, you can insist that every member of your family respects each other.

- *Expectations and boundaries* - Openly discuss parenting styles with your new partner *before* your family blends. Both parents must agree on discipline and look after all the children before combining families. And while you should set boundaries for your special child, know that he may not always adhere to the rules. However, it's essential to establish these boundaries and consistently reinforce them so that your special child learns to respect them over time. Do not remove the goalposts unless they are genuinely unattainable.

- *Family meetings* - Since everyone is adjusting to the new family, consider holding regular family meetings and allowing each member to speak their truth without fear of sanctions or being judged. This could be a time to openly talk about feelings, new family rules, activities, or anything else that needs to be discussed and shared.

- *Safety and security* - Since stepchildren have experienced losing a parent or separated birth parents, they need to feel safe and secure when their family blends. Avoid having arguments with your partner in the presence of your stepchildren. Arguments may remind them of the breakup of their biological family. And if they witness constant disagreements, it could lead them to be anxious or think that the stepfamily will dismantle.

- *Limit your expectations* - You might feel that you give plenty of love, time, attention, and energy to your partner's kids but receive very little in return. Don't be discouraged; consider the situation as an investment that will reap a bountiful harvest someday. Sure, it is exhausting for you to do all the right things only for the stepchildren to keep rejecting you and their new stepfamily. Nonetheless, if you are sincere, genuine, and consistent, the kids will witness and recognize how passionate you are.

Keep in mind that some disabilities affect the social skills of those diagnosed with them. So, the fact that your special stepchild does not appear to warm to you or does not return your affection does not automatically mean that he does not love and appreciate you. Once you understand your special child's condition and personality, you will be able to look beyond their behavior and let love reign in your household.

- *New experiences* - Build new memories as you experience new events or activities together. For instance, paint the house together, play games or participate in various sports, go on family picnics, or take family trips. It is beneficial to the family if you search for activities that can create new and pleasant memories for all the children.

Consider capturing photos of your new blended family. Have them framed, then place or hang them in the living room. Entering a stepfamily calls for endurance, creativity, and hard work. Time allocation is an invaluable factor in developing positive bonds in your stepfamily. Patience is indispensable.

Preserving your Individuality

While your purpose is to create a healthy and happy stepfamily, this does not mean that you shouldn't look after yourself anymore and just focus on the needs of your stepfamily. You must remain true to yourself and your values. Don't forget who you are as you try to blend with your new stepfamily. Caring for a special child can be all-consuming. It is easy to find yourself in a routine where you are constantly engaged in your caring role, losing sight of time and space as you fulfill his every need. Remember that you are an individual. Set aside time to enjoy your own company and reconnect with yourself.

You must also allow all your stepchildren to be their true selves, provided they do not get involved in things that could destroy, threaten, or make their lives and relationships with everyone difficult. Empower your special child to explore and experiment within reason. For example, maybe you can allow him to choose his gear or his toys. Below are some ideas as to how you can preserve individuality in your stepfamily.

- *Make yourself a priority* - Self-care is vital when you are in a relationship or entering a new stepfamily. Even though you have other people to take care of, you should also look after yourself.

Self-care comes in many different forms, such as remaining true to your preferences and goals in life, pursuing your passions, and doing what you love. You should not depend on another person to complete or fulfill you. We need to meet our own needs by remaining true to ourselves and what we love to do and achieve in life. Fulfillment could come from several different parts of our lives. For example, you can't achieve satisfaction solely by being married and having a family.

- *Be sure not to replace "I" with "We"* - Even if you are in a relationship or married to someone with kids, you shouldn't neglect your individuality. Regardless of how long you and your new partner have been together, you still must do things independently without them. For example, go out with friends, cook something that you love to eat for just yourself, and if you love pastries, don't say, "we love pastries." This indicates that you and your new partner and stepfamily share your preferences and interests. You must learn how to keep your identities separate from one another, even if you and your new partner think the same way most of the time.

- *Avoid over-compromising* - There is nothing wrong with compromising in a relationship. However, it is unhealthy if you're the only one who needs to make the sacrifices. You must learn when to bend in a relationship or marriage while also ensuring that you don't bend excessively to the point of breaking.

- *Make time to see your loved ones and friends* - While you are responsible for taking care of your new partner and stepchildren, you also have other people with whom you need to interact, including family and friends. Catching up with your favorite people *outside of your stepfamily* is healthy for you. They miss you as much as you miss them. Remember, your world does not merely revolve around your spouse and stepfamily.

- *Set boundaries* - The establishment of boundaries will aid you in sustaining your sense of self. Your boundaries safeguard who you are and protect your identity. Communicate your limits with your partner so they can respect them. Conflict accumulates over time if you don't set boundaries. You're more likely to feel exhausted, depleted, and sort of crushed. Healthy boundaries could help you feel more confident, assertive, and empowered within yourself or your relationship. It is utterly reasonable to have boundaries in your relationship, marriage, and family life. Each of us has things that we will and won't allow from another person. Remember that you don't have to sacrifice your boundaries just because you are in a relationship, married, or have a stepfamily.

- *Stay true to yourself* - There is no need for you to change who you are and be someone you are not. On the other hand, you don't need to fake it just to be accepted. Be honest and open with yourself and your partner about who you are. Ruminate on your present and past relationships. Have you sacrificed so much that you lost yourself in the long run? How can you reclaim yourself? Be confident and take ownership of who you are.

Your new partner should accept and love you regardless of who you are. They will be proud of you for staying true to yourself. Stepfamilies should respect each other's individuality. Even though you are one as a family, you still need to acknowledge and respect each other's differences, values, preferences, habits, and more.

Remind yourself that you deserve to be loved and accepted for who you are. There's no point in changing who you are in order to fit in.

Self-care in Blended Families

Stepparents need to acknowledge that self-care is important. Most of your time and energy will focus on your partner and the children when you have a family to raise. There are many simple ways to practice self-care. You can try listening to music, meditating, taking a long walk in a quiet place, doing yoga, and spending time with your favorite people. Below are some ideas on how to practice self-care.

- *Acknowledge your unique role - Never* think of yourself as a replacement parent. Instead, you need to be your stepchild's "special adult." This means you must be someone who can offer a trusted presence. You must always be willing to listen actively — a critical gesture that your stepchildren will appreciate. You aren't a replacement parent; you're someone who adds value to their family by living and loving and bonding the family unit.

- *Look for a trusted person you can talk to* - At times, it may be uncomfortable complaining to your spouse, who might be stubbornly loyal to their child. Consider finding a professional with more profound knowledge and expertise of the many pressures related to stepparenting children with special needs.

- *Keep your partnership strong* - You must be a strong unit that supports each other in all situations and with decision-making. Avoid training the children to resort to the other partner with the hope of achieving a better deal. Likewise, avoid altering the decisions made concerning your children without consulting your spouse. Instead, reach an agreement with your partner. From there, you can disclose your choices to the children involved. It is best if crucial decisions are communicated by both of you together to the children. Then, when the children know that both parents are in complete agreement, they won't try to manipulate each parent.

Special Dates

- *Give yourself a day off* - Whether it's a morning at your favorite coffee shop, enrolling in a course you like, working out at the gym, going to a hair salon or spa, or getting a relaxing massage, it's important to date yourself. Remind yourself that you deserve time off. Allow yourself to have "me time" and focus only on what you want to do. Your life does not need to revolve around your partner and other family members. You have a life to live, and you also have to take care of yourself to be in the best health to take care of others. Self-care is more about listening to yourself. You must listen to what your heart is telling you. Pay attention to your body and concentrate on yourself and the things you love to do alone or with others.

- *Spend quality time with your partner* - It is also essential to establish a solid and profound connection with your partner. (This is the notable distinction between first marriages and blending in a stepfamily.) It is crucial to make time for both of you. This will help you get to know each other well and deepen the bond between you.

Create memorable moments with each child - it is vital for you and your partner to have one-on-one time with each child. This activity will allow you to listen to each child, which could serve as a solid groundwork for a strong connection intently. It will also strengthen the bond between yourself and the child. This time is beneficial to children with special needs. It makes them feel loved and allows you to improve your understanding of your special stepchild.

Equality in Blended Families

Children tend to be inseparable from the parent who "stayed." And they often feel that anything they do might cause this biological parent to leave them. For example, if a parent left because they died, children might try to protect themselves from being hurt by dissociating themselves from the stepfamily.

Many adults in stepfamilies attempt to bring harmony and balance to their newly established blended family. They try to equate their new situation to their first relationship or marriage. Such a mindset will only lead to disappointment.

When blended families come together, children often attempt to determine whether they are welcome or function as part of the new system.

Tips for Achieving Equality in Your Stepfamily

- *Avoid competing with your partner* - You must recognize and respect the strength of the biological relationship. Be present in the life of your stepchild/children but refrain from competing with the birth parent. When a child with special needs is part of the stepfamily, the child's birth parent often feels more responsible for the care of that child. The birth parent often tends to assume most of the responsibility and essentially competes with the partner in matters relating to the child. Instead, the birth parent must recognize that they are part of a team and trust their partner to care for the child.

- *Defer the decisions for the stepchild to the bio-parent* - Even though the partners work as a team, the stepparent should recognize when to defer to the biological parent. Stepparents need to understand the importance of giving the step relationship some time to grow. This does not mean you'll completely vanish; it simply means that you must know when to step back and provide the stepparent with the necessary support (even if it goes against your parenting style). The more it seems to your stepchild that you and the bio-parent are in one accord, the better your connection with the stepchild will be.

- *Avoid interfering in private matters as much as possible* - Allow the bio-parent to have private time with their child. This lessens the loss and displacement the child might be feeling. It also assures the child that you have not replaced them. Some stepparents may get anxious if their partner has private time with their child and they're excluded. Remind yourself that this private time lets the birth parent enjoy their child. Such an approach will let the child know that the stepparent is not taking their birth parent away.

- *Become familiar with your stepchild's interests and preferences* - You should discover your stepchild's favorite activities. You can start by finding some common interests and then doing those things together.

- *Show love, even if you and your stepchild are not agreeing* - Even if you don't like the attitudes or behavior of your stepchild, you still should show love. It could be that your personalities clash, or you feel that they reject you. In a worst-case scenario, you both dislike each other; that happens. But you have to remember that you are the parent, and you have to take a mature stance. Children might not behave like their usual selves after a separation or remarriage of their parents. So, show love to your stepchildren, even when it hurts. Give them time to heal.

- *Search for what's good and right* - Rather than concentrating on the negative aspects or complaining about them, look for something positive to share or say to your partner. Such an approach puts your spouse in a positive mindset that will help you build a healthy bond with your stepchildren. This will also aid you in fostering a good bond between your kid and your stepchildren. When you are caring for a child with special needs, you may find yourself challenged pretty often. However, there will be moments of enjoyment that you should not ignore. Praise and reward good behavior and let your special child feel special when they display positive behavior.

Remember, healthy relationships require time to develop. They also call for a considerable amount of maturity, patience, perseverance, and commitment from all the adults involved. Treat your biological child and stepchildren equally and fairly. There should be no favoritism.

Encouraging Positivity in Stepchildren

As mentioned earlier, being in a relationship with someone who has children is potentially more challenging than marrying a single partner. When one or more of those children has a disability, the challenges multiply, and the stepparent may find him or herself on a steep learning curve. Stepparenting is a process. Before living together, acknowledge this process and prepare for the journey. Disciplining your stepchildren can be more challenging than disciplining your child.

Love, trust, and emotional attachment are vital factors that underlie good parenting. The tone of your voice when talking to the child is critical here. Concentrate on how it makes you feel. And make it a point to assure the child that you are willing to listen and talk about any issues they have with you.

As most of us know, relationships without rules can be chaotic. Children in these types of environments are more likely to become rebellious. Smart stepparents have a deeper understanding of this, and they develop strategies to establish authority in their stepfamilies. As a stepparent, you initially act as an extension of the bio-parent, and it is your role to build positivity in your stepfamily.

Avoid any negative talk about the absent parent and talk instead about events and new ideas. If your stepchild talks negatively about you with their absent parent, discuss this privately with your partner and allow the biological parent to have private time with the child. After that, you, your partner, and the child can openly discuss the matter together.

It is often said that "Love makes the world go round". Chapter 2 demonstrates that a stepfamily built on love will weather many storms. When this key ingredient is nurtured and combined with an attitude of forgiveness and support, the stepfamily will thrive. Open and honest communication, fairness, respect for individual space, empathy and quality family time and are factors that are key to promoting a stable, happy and thriving stepfamily.

A Short Anecdote

Danny's mom, Sarah, was accompanying Danny to a medical appointment in another state. Danny has Tourette syndrome, and his mom was anxious about the long bus journey. Danny's stepfather, Jonathan, and Sarah divorced three years ago, but Jonathan would check periodically on Danny. When Jonathan called, Danny told him of the impending trip and asked if he could accompany them. Jonathan knew that Sarah found these trips stressful, so he offered his help. Sarah was thrilled to receive the support for the journey. Unfortunately, Danny's biological dad said that he was unavailable as he had to go to work.

This short story is a manifestation of a strong foundation of love in a stepfamily. We might not be blood-related, but love binds us all.

Chapter 3

LISTENING

"In order to move forward, sometimes you've got to stand still"

Communication is vital to maintaining a healthy, happy stepfamily. For that reason, you must listen to your stepchildren. It would help if you learned the significance between listening and merely hearing what they say.

Children who are non-verbal have a point to make, too. The stepfamily must understand how they communicate and create opportunities to express their sentiments, make choices, and participate in family decisions. It is not good enough to assume that they have nothing to say or that the options do not matter. Promote effective communication by ensuring that all members of the stepfamily have a chance to be heard. This means compromising, actively listening, conducting conversations calmly and respectfully, and providing effective feedback. All these key factors will help you solve various problems in the family. Stepparents are responsible for promoting the significance of listening to one another.

Communication in Blended Families

Frequent and open communication with your stepchild is indispensable. How the members of a blended family connect and correspond with each other says a lot about trust between the family members. When communication is open, transparent, and frequent, misunderstandings are less likely to emerge. This helps provide more possibilities for connections between stepparents and stepchildren.

Stepparents need to discuss everything that pertains to the child with the stepchild. Uncertainties and concerns regarding various family problems result from poor communication. That's why communication must be as open and frequent as possible. Avoid holding grudges and repressing your emotions; always address any pressing issues early. Listen and build a non-judgmental and open atmosphere at home that allows everyone to be heard.

Stepparents can easily and comfortably provide opportunities for effective communication by doing activities together with stepchildren. For example, when there are issues or matters that you need to discuss with your stepchildren, consider playing sports or games or doing activities with them. Then, during the activity, you will have a perfect opportunity to start the conversation, which helps avoid any awkward feelings. Remember, stepchildren are generally sensitive. So, the words you use when discussing some things with them are *significant*. Be sure to use considerate and respectful language with each other.

To maintain harmony even when talking about uncomfortable topics, avoid insulting remarks, name-calling, and using annoying words to incite arguments. Also, stepparents can consider mealtime as a perfect platform for discussing various concerns. Mealtimes can serve as the ideal scenario for establishing a meaningful and cordial conversation. Just be careful not to overdo it—you don't want your children dreading mealtimes.

Encourage your stepchild to learn how to speak up properly, defend or support viewpoints, and listen intently even to opposing opinions. Your special child may communicate differently. The entire family must be encouraged to pay attention to him, irrespective of how long he may take to make a point or communicate via body language. You will teach your neurotypical stepchildren to be patient, empathetic, and respectful if you lead by example. They have an excellent opportunity to develop good interpersonal skills when they share a home with a special child who needs support. Stepchildren will also greatly appreciate it when they see their stepparents determined to make their blended family a haven where everyone is loved, accepted, and supported.

Always allow stepchildren to express their thoughts. Encourage them to talk freely about their needs, wishes, and dreams without the fear of being shut down, ridiculed, or rejected.

Lastly, biological parents and stepparents must devote family time to their children. It gets somewhat more difficult when the children become teenagers and want to spend more time with their friends. Nowadays, they also have access to various screens where they can interact with friends. So, even if they are home, they might be chatting to friends and only giving you their partial attention. While you will need to allow some of this to happen, do not lose sight of your child. Negotiate family and one-on-one time with the child, letting them have a say in the decisions made around this.

Avoid serious conflicts and resentment with your stepchild by not being too draconian with the rules. Let love and understanding be the foundation of your relationship with your stepchild. One-on-one time with a parent is one area where children with special needs may be easier to manage. They often crave more attention from their parents, partly because of their dependence on them and also because they have limited access to friends and gadgets they can control.

Recognizing the Losses of your Stepchildren

No matter the age, children experience the effects of a loss after the divorce or death of parents or a parent. Unfortunately, most adults fail to acknowledge this because they are too absorbed with their losses and personal issues. While it's true that it is normal for people to focus on their losses rather than someone else's, stepparents must recognize the effects of the loss on their stepchildren. Since your kids are still young, they lack maturity, and their coping skills are not fully developed.

When children feel heard, the burdens of their loss are somewhat alleviated. This happens because they realize they're not alone and discover that someone is willing to listen to them. Having someone they can talk to when they need it can make a big difference in handling new situations or transitions.

Respect in Stepfamilies

Respect is not only about the children's behavior toward the adults in the blended family. It must be given regardless of age, and it should also be based on the reality that you are now a family. In all types of relationships, members of blended families should highly regard and respect each member's rights, wishes, and feelings.

Children with learning disabilities are equally deserving of respect. That means your neurotypical stepchild should not be allowed to invade or disrupt your child's space or speak when the other child is communicating. In general, they should not be allowed to be disrespectful in any way.

While there's no denying that the love between stepparents and stepchildren is not automatic, respectful behavior can serve to make a positive initial impression. Being respectful can undoubtedly make a remarkable difference in the first few weeks, months, and years.

People consider stepchildren who respect their stepparents as properly taught kids with good manners. On the other hand, many people think that stepchildren who act rudely and disrespect their stepparents are not taught proper manners. However, children may behave differently despite growing up in the same household. Some kids choose to be respectful, while others act rudely even when their biological parents teach them the difference between right and wrong.

Stepparents who do not understand the intricacies of the disability of their stepchild may think that they are disrespectful when, in actuality, they are simply demonstrating the effects of their diagnosis. This is why stepparents must gain knowledge through research, questioning, observation, reading, and other media, or by joining groups to learn from those who have experience and expertise in the area.

Though you may have parented other children, it is vital to recognize the uniqueness of your special stepchild. The onus is on *you* to learn what you can to understand him. One of the lessons I learned during my search for knowledge was to adjust my expectations. I discovered that I must adapt my parenting and teaching methodology to accommodate the child's personality.

Often the negative behaviors that the child displays are not entirely in his control. This is true for some conditions more than others, and it doesn't mean that you should refrain from teaching your child the correct behavior. Do not assume that he cannot learn. Instead, model good behavior and offer tangible and intangible rewards when you are rewarded with good behavior.

Some kids demonstrate rudeness because it is their way of expressing their dislike for a transition. Their lack of respect might signify their confusion, agony, or sadness at what is happening to their family circumstances. Sometimes, it may also be their way of demonstrating loyalty to their biological parents.

Children generally learn respect and disrespect from observing how adults treat them and others. Put simply, children usually mimic what they see adults do and say. They are watching you even when you don't see it, so it is vital always to be a model for appropriate behavior. One way to demonstrate respect is by regulating your tone of voice when discussing issues with your stepchildren. You can show respect by allowing your stepchildren to have time alone with their biological parents and respecting their privacy.

Offering support and encouraging stepchildren are ways of showing them that you respect or appreciate them. You and your partner should discuss your expectations for respect; they must be expressed, shared, and shown to everyone in the stepfamily. This is particularly crucial when living arrangements change. Including these habits will go a long way in establishing a harmonious relationship within your stepfamily.

Compassion-focused Stepparenting

One thing is sure: the members of your stepfamily will be at different stages in their lives. They will have different needs, and they might embrace your new family differently. For these reasons, family members need to understand and honor each other's differences. Stepparents have a role to play in modeling patience. They must also teach the children in the family unit to avoid being overly sensitive to comments and behaviors of others.

Empathy and compassion are two crucial ingredients for loving relationships, successful marriages, and parenthood. Parents can empathize with their children by recognizing that they live in a different era. They can also show empathy by adjusting to their long-held beliefs so children can have a nurturing and safe space at home. Empathy encourages you to support family members with special needs and spend quality time with them. Your level of compassion and empathy may range from comforting a crying baby to encouraging a spouse who is anxious about an upcoming court date surrounding a custody battle.

Empathy is one of the key components to humanity's longevity. It makes human connections stick together. The reality is that we cannot survive without connecting with others. It would be far more challenging if we had no one to empathize with us when situations get tough.

Stepparents must be sensitive to the needs and distress of their stepchildren to be able to respond accordingly. Compassion for blended family members, particularly stepchildren, means you are sensitive to the suffering of others. And you are committed to doing your best to lessen or prevent the suffering.

Being compassionate with children is highly important because parental neglect can cause behavioral issues that affect relationships. Children will learn innumerable life lessons, but there also comes a time when you cannot allow the child to suffer and cope with anxieties alone. If a situation appears to be "breaking" them, it is not time for you to increase pressure and be judgmental. As a stepparent, you have nothing to prove.

Compassion also calls for action. You must understand your family members, be open, and appropriately respond to sympathy from others. Compassion-focused parenting is not solely about alleviating threats and suffering in a child's surroundings. It's about granting the opportunity for kids to explore. It is also about allowing them to grow socially, emotionally, and behaviorally.

The actions I mentioned above are more effective when parents are secure. When parents feel uncertain and threatened, they tend to engage skeptically and are more likely to respond imprudently. But please be aware that being a compassionate stepparent does not only mean kindness to your stepchildren. You also need to keep them out of trouble, and for that, moments of tough love might be appropriate. Don't be afraid to be firm with your special child. Many of these children are extremely clever and will manipulate you.

I recall visiting a friend with an autistic child some years ago. The boy, who is high-functioning autistic, poured a glass of water on the table. When I asked him why he had done that, he said, "Because of my autism." I am not an autism specialist, but I felt that the boy understood that what he had done was unacceptable. Stepparents must be compassionate without enabling negative behavior.

If your family uses sanctions for your neurotypical children, you should consider doing the same for your special child. Do not reward or encourage negative behavior; instead, model appropriate behavior and reward them for it. I know a family in our parent group who has a child with ADHD. She said the child, who is only seven, breaks every toy and has broken three laptops and two iPads. An appropriate sanction, in that case, would be to limit his access to the items and allow him to use them only under supervision.

Stepparenting can sometimes feel like a chore. Stepparents are more likely to have higher stress, self-doubt, and guilt levels as they consider the best and most effective ways of fulfilling their roles. When a special child is part of the household, those sentiments escalate. Children with physical disabilities who need assistance are just as challenging as those with cognitive disabilities who demonstrate stubbornness.

I have a friend with a child with challenging behavior, and she often has to 'fight' her 12-year-old son to get ready for school. Three out of five mornings per week, she has to take him to school herself because he refuses to get ready in time for the bus. In those instances, you might not feel like being compassionate, but really, you must. Being a compassionate stepparent calls for capabilities and competencies not required from typical parents.

Showing compassion involves understanding what your stepchild is going through. Yes, it can be difficult to show compassion when you are distressed about a situation. But recognizing and valuing your stepchild's feelings could serve as a dynamic means to help create stronger connections.

When you're compassionate, you make children feel that you understand they are going through something, even if you don't completely understand how it feels to them. Without fail, this message is valuable for children to hear. When children feel supported and understood, they get motivated. Your empathy and compassion can also help them be courageous enough to voice what they need and become more aware of themselves.

Compassion-focused parenting can serve as a powerful instrument in helping you understand what's behind the behavior. It could aid you and your child in collaborating and addressing challenges as they arise. This connection could also help you through tough times.

The Power of Active Listening

Active listening is a must in blended families. It enables stepparents to empower their stepchildren in exploring their feelings and thoughts on a more profound level. It also substantially helps stepparents develop a deeper understanding of the child and build empathy. Best of all, active listening can work as an effective instrument in enhancing communication and establishing a healthy connection with your stepchild.

The Fundamentals of Active Listening

As previously discussed, active listening is not just about hearing what someone is saying. It is a skill that you need to master. To listen actively, you must:

- Give your children the utmost attention
- Concentrate on what your child is saying instead of thinking about what you will say next
- Get close to the child when they are voicing their concerns
- Show your child that you are willing and interested in listening (i.e., make comments, use sign language, nod your head, etc.)
- Refrain from asking questions that could ruin the child's train of thought
- Make eye contact to show that your child is being heard and understood
- Let the child speak without interrupting them
- Ask questions in a way that the child understands
- Offer choices to non-verbal children and those who do not have the required vocabulary to express their wishes.

Please note that listening is not the same as agreeing. It is possible to respect and understand someone's opinions without consenting to them.

The Advantages of Active Listening

To a large extent, a valuable component of a healthy and robust connection is open and honest communication. For communication to be successful, it will primarily rely on how you listen. You can intensify your communication by actively listening and thus solidifying your relationship with your stepchildren. This will demonstrate to your child that you are interested and concerned.

Active listening does not require much talking on your part. You won't be forced to come up with answers to resolve issues at once, which makes it more possible for your stepchild to ask you what you think about what he is saying. When your child has challenges surrounding speech or learning, you should prompt them and encourage them to talk to you.

It's beneficial for your child's thinking process to discuss matters with you. Have conversations regularly, even if you think the child is not listening or cannot sustain meaningful discussions. Use sign language or body language to elicit information. If you know that the child would like a particular object, put it out of reach, so he must ask you for it. Use the item to spark conversation—talk about the color, shape, taste, or feel of it, and if you have the time, spend some time engaging with the child using it. Help them think more clearly and develop an understanding of the context of your conversations.

Generally speaking, good listening is an excellent means of demonstrating to your stepchildren that you care and are interested in listening to them. Active listening is also a powerful tool in inhibiting conflicts.

How to Improve your Active Listening Skills

- *Listen intently* - Listening intently implies that you pay complete attention to the speaker. If you feel like your mind is starting to wander, you must do your best to bring it back to the topic. When your stepchild talks to you, don't use gadgets or devices that detract from the conversation. Focus on him and indicate that he is a priority. Show him you are willing to provide time and that you're interested in what he's feeling, thinking, and doing.

- *Understand what is being said* - Focus on what your stepchild is saying, and don't be distracted by what you're going to say next. If you think of what to say next, you'll miss what the child is saying.

- *Demonstrate to your stepchild that you are trying to understand* - Consider summing up your child's primary points as well as what you perceive he might be feeling. Alternatively, you can repeat what he is saying using your own words. Avoid being judgmental and do not intertwine irrelevant facts into the current conversation.

Chapter 3 reminds us that blended families can achieve happiness, harmony, and fulfillment amidst boundless challenges in the journey. Stepparents must remember that immediate adjustment is unrealistic. They need to listen to their children to experience a more rewarding journey. Building a stepfamily is a significant life change for everyone, so flexibility is critical for success.

A Short Anecdote

Sarah is almost 18 and has learning difficulties. Her mother died when she was 12, and Sarah lived with her aunt for a year. Her father remarried, and Sarah went back to live with him and her stepmother, Mary. Sarah's father died last year. Shortly after, Mary had to go into a home for the elderly. She was not allowed to take Sarah with her. They see each other every fortnight and speak on the phone almost daily. Sarah shares every secret, and Mary is always there to listen.

Having someone who listens intently is invaluable to a child with special needs. Genuine friends are harder to find, and having this bond with her stepmother is a real safety blanket for Sarah. Mary looks forward to the calls from Sarah, too; they brighten up her day and alleviate her from the monotony of living with older adults.

Though there were miles between them, the distance did not separate them, and they could make time and space for each other to their mutual benefit. Their bond stretches past a simple family/friends relationship. This anecdote reveals how crucial open communication and active listening is, specifically in blended families.

Chapter 4

LAUGHING

"One day we come to realize what's truly important in life; it's not money, the job or stuff. It's people!"

It is no secret that laughing, spending quality time together, and creating happy moments can make the adjustment period less burdensome for everyone. Though the journey to a happy stepfamily is often not a smooth sailing process, it can be achieved by embedding laughter and fun into the process.

Adaptability is one of the primary attributes of healthy, loving, and lasting blended family relationships. Creating opportunities for fun will work wonders for making the bond within the blended family more substantial and profound.

Family Celebrations

Blended families can incorporate celebrations for minor and major milestones. These need not be grand and pricey, but they do need to be inclusive. Do not be deterred if your family is on a budget; you can be creative and find ways around this. For example, instead of purchasing an expensive cake, you can make this a family project and have everyone assist in baking cupcakes at home. You can look online or in cookbooks for easy recipes. Finding ways for the entire family to plan celebrations, even in simple ways, will strengthen the family bond.

Besides birthdays, take time to celebrate other accomplishments of each member of your stepfamily. When your special child makes himself a sandwich for the first time, celebrate that. In that case, celebrating could simply mean the family clapping and praising the child. You could also reward him with tangible or intangible gifts that make him feel special. Small, frequent celebrations are excellent for recognizing achievements, building closeness, and instilling confidence.

These mini celebrations with stepfamily members are essential for your special stepchild. It is well-documented that children with special needs generally receive fewer invitations to parties. Some families find it stressful to participate in social gatherings because they cannot handle the noise or the journey. The family may also find it difficult because of stigma or other social and environmental issues. While this is the case, every effort must be made to ensure that your special stepchild has his fair share of the outside world.

Fun Activities in the Home

Turn your home into a fun zone! Make fun and laughter an integral part of your life. Irrespective of any medical conditions in the family, do not lose joy in the home. If a man's home is his castle, the man must be happy in his home. Do your best to secure indoor and outdoor toys and activity centers (e.g. trampolines, tricycles, and board games) for the entire family to enjoy. Some children with special needs enjoy playing with items around the house. They may choose a pot and a spoon to emulate the sound of a drum. My daughter was particularly good at using household items to play music. She often ignored the musical instruments she had at her disposal.

If you have a garden or open space at home, encourage your children to use it. Buy a skipping rope, or a scooter, or other items that will promote play and happiness in your family. Ensure that your special child is part of every activity (though you may need to keep an eye on him if he is using shared space). We are lucky enough to have a private garden, but we also have a shared space where children can play. We had the experience of a child hitting our little girl for no reason; perhaps he didn't like the look of her. Luckily, I was watching and was able to address the situation quickly. The matter of bullying is always a concern, so keep an extra eye on your special child when he's interacting with other children.

Another way of engendering fun in the home is to turn household chores into fun-filled activities by incorporating play. Assign tasks to each child or team. Use the opportunity to teach. For example, sort utensils into different drawers, or containers into different colors, arrange plates into grooves according to size, name the utensils, etc. Some children with special needs find these activities difficult, and by taking the chance to do these chores, a stepparent is improving the child's motor and life skills.

Be patient with your special child—they may not follow instructions as keenly as others. That may mean you have to ask him more than once, and at times you will have to help them ensure a task is accomplished. Never assume that the child does not understand or is unable to comply with your instructions. Admit that it can be exhausting to repeat the same instructions; but do not relent. Your child must not be made to feel that he gets to do nothing because of his diagnosis. Your child is not his diagnosis; he is an individual with a diagnosis.

If you have a garden, ask the children to help you eliminate the weeds, re-pot plants, water them, or do other DIY landscaping projects. You have to be vigilant when working in the garden with your special child. Some children will put anything into their mouths, and you may turn around to find his mouth filled with earth. Avoid using fertilizers or chemicals around the child. Some of our children are non-verbal and may not be able to articulate what they did or where it hurts. There are various creative and fun-filled household chores you could explore.

Another way to enjoy your home is to find ways of filling your lives with sweet surprises. "Sweet surprises" does not mean spending lavishly on expensive gifts for your new partner and children. If you are resourceful and creative, you can do it yourself. For instance, write a thank you note and put it inside your partner's bag or pocket. Or make lunch boxes with surprise items that make the child smile. If you're good at crafting or completing other creative projects like designing a wooden toy for your special child, you can also do that. Of course, if there are other kids in the family, you will need to do the same for them.

Fun Activities outside the Home

Families that play together have stronger relationships and share closer values. There are many fun family outdoor activities that family members of all ages can enjoy in all seasons.

When thinking about stepfamily activities outside the home, consider each family member's preferences and ensure that they have a turn. Your special child may like to go to the mall and have ice cream, while a neurotypical child may prefer to see a movie. In that case, you can go to the mall as a family and have ice cream one day; then another day go to see a movie. You will need to have compromise, as some movies are not suitable for some children. And if your special child finds it difficult to keep quiet, it will be better to choose an autism-friendly movie for the entire family to attend. Treating teenagers to hot chocolate in a coffee shop or attending their favorite sports game are other popular choices for family activities.

When you are out with your special child, you must be vigilant and spot dangers that may not be evident to others. For example, some time ago, our family attended a social event. My daughter was seated on my right, and an elderly lady occupied the seat next to her. Someone brought a cup of tea to the lady, and she started to sip the tea. This was an innocent gesture, but instantly I could see the danger, and I immediately exchanged seats with my daughter. I knew that all it would take was for the child to move awkwardly, and the hot beverage would be spilled, burning those nearby.

In today's modern world, almost all of us are already aware that multiple types of families exist. Same-sex families are on the rise, and more and more children find loving, safe spaces in these families. You can alter the public's view of what families look like by celebrating your stepfamily. Doing so could overcome the stigma that has haunted blended families and other unacknowledged family structures for years.

When your stepfamily includes a child with special needs, you may feel excluded from certain activities in society. Attitudes are changing about people with special needs and disabilities, but there are still those who think it necessary to jeer disabled people and make them feel inhuman. This hurts not only the child, but the entire family. By participating in celebrations, you will be playing your part to resist and eradicate stigma. Though we want to think that we are not affected by people's comments, actions, and inactions, the truth is, no one is invulnerable to negativity. Sticks and stones can break bones, and words can hurt too. Celebrations can reduce uncertainties that some family members might be experiencing.

Family adventures and excursions are another way of having fun with your stepfamily. When your blended family includes a child with special needs, you need a more detailed game plan. You'll have to research the facilities carefully to ensure suitability for your special child. Some children do not tolerate noise or crowds very well. If your child's medication needs to be kept in the refrigerator, you will need to figure out how to accommodate it. If you are staying in a basic bed and breakfast area, you must ask about the facilities. Find out about access to the site if your child struggles with stairs.

Stepfamilies that play together develop strong relationships. There are many other fun family outdoor activities that family members of all ages can enjoy across all seasons. If you are a stepparent who understands your stepchild, you should know how the child can participate in different activities. Their capabilities depend on their ability to walk, their tolerance of specific activities (for example, some children will find it difficult to climb into a canoe), and other peculiarities based on their diagnosis. Following are some outdoor activities that you may consider for your family.

- *Camping* - Camping is a popular activity for families. You can make an excursion to a campsite or do it in the backyard.

- *Family picnic* - On a warm, sunny day, you can hold a family picnic in your local park. Pack a blanket and your family's favorite snacks and head outdoors to dine al fresco.

- *Hiking* - A family hike is a fun activity and great exercise. You can investigate nature trails and parks and discover breathtaking sights.

- *Birdwatching* - This is an easy and entertaining activity for all family members. Depending on where you live, you may pick up a field guide from a local bookstore or library, see how many bird species you can find in your neighborhood, and keep a list of the birds you come across.

- *Fishing* - Get some fishing rods, bait, and snacks, and head out to the local lake. You should first check to see if you are allowed to fish at the spot before setting out. Even if you don't catch anything, kids will have fun learning to be patient and catch fish. Should you get lucky and catch a fish or two, capture the images on camera or video and create lasting memories.

- *Watersports* - Renting a kayak or canoe is a fun family activity. Explore a local lake or river, or make it part of a camping trip. Follow all safety precautions, including the wearing of life jackets. Other great watersports for the family include river rafting, fishing, boating, water skiing, and swimming. In the winter, you can participate in sledding, skiing, tubing, ice skating, and snowboarding.

- *Biking* - Bike rides are environmentally friendly and great exercise for everyone. Ensure that the bikes are in good condition and everyone wears a helmet. A significant number of children with special needs find it difficult to balance on a bicycle. You can compensate for this by using special tricycles designed for these children. Combine biking with a picnic to double the fun.

- *Festivals and fairs* - Periodic outdoor festivals can provide great fun for the family. Hot-air balloon festivals, county fairs, organized nature walks, fireworks shows, and kite flying festivals are all options.

- *Days at the beach* - Beach days are fantastic for families. You can swim, surf, or play beach games like Frisbee and volleyball. Children can search for seashells and build sandcastles. Families may choose to have a picnic and take a stroll along the beach.

Other outdoor activities may be available for your family. For instance, there may be trampoline parks, play centers, and other options near you. Just remember, the idea here is to have fun with the *entire* family outside the home.

When you are planning excursions with your blended family, there is one area that you may need to negotiate: dates with the other biological parent. Depending on the circumstances of your family, the other biological parent might have an agreed-upon parenting schedule. That means your proposed time away may infringe on those dates.

Some families can quickly sort this issue, but some separations are acrimonious and prove far more complex. I recall the challenges of a friend and her ex-husband who have two children with special needs. She wanted to have three weeks away with her new partner and his daughter. The ex-husband and his family took her to court, asserting that she would move abroad with the children.

It was a very stressful time for her. She convinced the court that this was not the case, then proceeded on her holiday and returned as planned with her children. Ensure that your ex-partner is aware and agrees in writing for you to take the children away on holidays. Figuring out schedules with the co-parent can be distressing and challenging. It is not always easy to secure alternative dates. So, when there are conflicting schedules, choose another available date and avoid the stresses of fighting with your ex-partner.

One of the first conversations to have with your new partner is to discuss parenting arrangements for both of your sets of children. These may change as the children get older but are still important to establish in the early days, especially if your ex-partner is abusive or prone to violence or spite.

The delightful news is that there are uncountable fun-filled outdoor activities for blended families. Just remember not to make promises that you cannot keep. If canceling a pre-arranged activity turns out to be inevitable, make up for it by rescheduling.

Blended families that play together have more profound, stronger connections. The central message here is to have fun together with your blended family. There is no need to break the bank. There are limitless family get-togethers that you can consider without the need to spend excessive amounts of money. Remember, sincere words and loving actions are far better than material items. Everyone appreciates tangible gifts, but sentiments of love and loving actions are priceless and worth remembering.

Celebrations provide opportunities for communication in the stepfamily and with members of the extended family. When celebrations are successful, they can improve relationships, which is good for the mental well-being of parents and their children.

Tips for Successful Celebrations

- *Create a schedule in advance* - If you plan a trip, each parent and child should have a copy of the schedule. If your special child cannot read the schedule, consider creating a storyboard with visual aids to represent each step. Remember, never ignore your special child, and don't assume they will not comprehend what you are saying or doing. Once the schedule is formulated, try to follow it. Issues such as train delays or effects from bad weather are out of your control, but just try to respect the schedule as much as you can. This will make it easier for your special child to follow.

- *Build new traditions and respect current ones* - As you establish new blended family traditions, you also need to recognize other traditions or practices with due respect. Remember that you were all part of two separate families with distinctive customs and celebrations. Be aware of and respect your stepchildren's traditions with their biological parents and family. Then, strive harder to combine those traditions into your new celebrations.

Celebrating occasions as a stepfamily can evoke different emotions. But by respecting other traditions, you can create the best celebrations with your stepfamily.

- *Manage expectations* - Remember that reality may not match every expectation you and your blended family might have. Avoid committing to specific outcomes such as a "flawless" holiday. Instead, when things change, explain to your stepchildren what is happening and maintain a light mood even if you are concerned. Making your children worry will not help. Fun is essential for a fulfilled life, and the best place to get started is at home. The following paragraphs present some fun-filled and cost-effective tips to have fun with your stepfamily.

- *Celebrating milestones* - Birthdays, weddings, holidays, and other significant occasions are not the only milestones you need to celebrate. It is also essential to celebrate minor accomplishments. For instance, you can make ordinary days and weekends memorable. Turn a Saturday or Sunday into a family picnic or "get-together" day. Be creative. Involve everyone in preparing for the celebrations. Create a role for your special child and let them work with others in the family to complete their task. By doing so, you are building confidence, competence, and social skills.

- *Events* - Allow the children in your blended family to attend events where they can interact with people outside their family unit. Where possible, allow them to participate in activities and occasions with classmates and friends. Let them participate in school outings and other events organized by groups equipped to take care of them. For example, my daughter attended a Catholic school and was one of three students invited and taken to France on a pilgrimage. The pictures and videos they sent me showed that she had a lot of fun while building her confidence and learning new skills.

- *Educational trips* - Children can join local educational trips to explore their surroundings and visit museums and other historical sites. These activities are excellent means for them to establish connections and make friends. We know that people's lives do not solely revolve around their families. Children can learn more about building friendships and dealing with other people when you let them spend time with others. Doing so can expand the family support network as well. Families of disabled children are good sources of information and support to similar families.

Socialization is a vital part of everyone's life. The adults and the children in a stepfamily need to socialize as they journey through life. We *all* need to socialize with other people aside from our family. Doing so allows us to discover and learn more about our environment. Parents need to allow their children to learn how to interact with others to communicate and socialize appropriately.

Your special child has equal rights to socializing, as do your other children. Sometimes you will need to identify special clubs for the child to join and attend. But, do not feel obligated to confine your child to events for children with special needs. Try to let them mingle with neurotypical children who model typical behaviors.

Depending on the severity of your child's disability, remember to pack extra gear for them. Ensure that the caregivers are aware of any special care requirements. In some instances, the host institution may need to conduct an assessment during which they will collect information about your child to ensure his health and safety while in their care. You may need to document step-by-step instructions if the child is spending an extended period away from home. Never leave your child with anyone who doesn't understand his medical needs.

As biological parents or stepparents, you must allow your children to play with other kids, spend time with their classmates and friends, etc. Letting the children in your blended family socialize is excellent for helping them develop social skills and life skills that will assist them in succeeding throughout life. They will learn how to be independent, and their communication skills will improve. They can also learn the significance of respect, friendship, sharing, and humility. All these strengths enable kids to better adapt to various situations and deal with others.

Socialization will also teach the children how to manage different issues like discrimination, bullying, and rejection. Stepparents need to understand that even though you would like to protect your special child as much as you can, it isn't possible to do so forever. And if you are more open to exposing your children to the real world, you will be glad to see them enjoying life outside your home.

Most of us are aware that life consists of highs and lows. Young children will learn this life lesson when they get emotionally and physically hurt. It's natural for this to happen as they develop and mature. Your special child will have his peculiar way of showing pain, and you, as parents and stepparents, will recognize these signals.

If your child is non-verbal, you will need to be eagle-eyed to ensure they are not seriously hurt. And you *must* provide moral support when your children get hurt. This support will help boost their confidence so they can move forward and avoid any lasting damage.

Parents normally overprotect their special children. While these children do require extra protection, the aim is not to deny them the opportunity to learn maneuvers independently. One learns valuable skills through pain, and while you want to minimize these stinging pains, you can't eliminate them. It is almost impossible for your child to spend every waking hour with you. They must learn skills that empower them to overcome challenges while growing up. Overprotecting your child is more likely denying them an opportunity to develop competence and independence.

Being a stepparent of a special child requires proactivity. You can help your child socialize by forming a group among your wider family and friends and arranging weekly meetups. You may want to meet in different locations and engage in other activities.

You can choose sites like the local park, playground, picnic areas, or even at the home of one of the families. Choose settings that are large enough for your children to run around. As parents of a special child, you might find this to be a tedious process. Some families of neurotypical children are not patient and may not want to participate in this plan as their children are more independent.

You have to be patient and persistent when teaching your child to socialize because not all children can quickly develop social skills. It may take several attempts. What works for my family is for my special child to video-call her friend and say hello. If your child is non-verbal, you can still try this technique. This is not an attempt to teach speech and language skills; instead, it builds social skills.

Interaction with Nature

Aside from socializing with others, stepparents need to help the children in their stepfamily appreciate their surroundings. A walk in the park or a visit to the farm can be fun and help keep your children grounded. You implement games and use the opportunity to teach important life lessons in the process.

There are countless ways you can use nature to teach children valuable life lessons. For instance, planting trees, gardening, tree-hugging, and cleaning up surroundings are simple acts, yet they can instill essential life lessons and be fun.

The Benefits of Interacting with Nature

According to research, nature has a positive effect on our well-being. This includes having fewer physical illnesses, psychological well-being, faster recovery from various ailments, and improved cognitive functions.

Our planet provides boundless opportunities for creativity, education, discovery, and problem-solving. Connecting with our natural environment enables kids to explore by experimenting and working on ideas. Nature also dramatically improves our sense of serenity. Various research papers have uncovered that interacting with nature can significantly lessen the symptoms of anxiety and ADHD.

- *Social benefits* - This is linked to the socialization discussed earlier. When kids play in nature, they can socialize with other children in their age groups and can participate in games that include more people. When your child has a disability, you have to watch him as he interacts with other children. And if your child is non-verbal, you should ensure that he is safe among children who are not members of your household.

Kids can interact with others or play alone in nature. They can learn, problem-solve, and share with others. When interacting with nature, kids commonly collaborate to create activities and orders since there are no required sets of rules.

When exploring outdoors, kids learn how to create their own rules and look for solutions on their own because adults are not with them. They learn how to stand on their own two feet. It's a great way of teaching them not to always depend on someone to do things for them. As a result, active and challenging kids might calm down and become gentler when exposed to nature. Kids may also learn how to reach out and develop empathy.

- *Physical benefits* - The fresh air of nature is uplifting and invigorating. It provides limitless opportunities to enjoy physical activities. Such activities help build stronger, recharged bodies. As parents or stepparents, it is your job to provide a reasonable balance of safety and risk. Make sure you give some degree of challenge to your kids so they can freely master new sets of skills.

- *Environmental benefits* - Our children are future stewards of the natural environment. So, parents must teach their kids how to love, appreciate, and care for Mother Earth. Enable their connection to nature by liberating them and letting them dig into the wonderment and marvel of our planet.

Chapter 4 shows that laughter is a therapeutic instrument that helps stepparents and stepchildren create a positive and happy blended family environment. To sustain happiness and harmony in your blended family, make laughter indispensable to achieving those goals. Laughter relieves stress, lightens the mood, and works wonders in helping us maintain perspective. It also establishes stronger connections and creates beautiful memories.

A Short Anecdote

The Blake stepfamily makes it a priority to have get-togethers on weekends if everyone's schedule allows it. This blended family enjoys cycling around North Portland's

Parkways. The biological mother and stepdad enable the children to play with their friends as well. Whenever they go cycling, two of their children's friends join them.

The same goes for when they have a picnic. The terms "step" and "ex" are not in the vocabulary of the Blake stepfamily. Instead, their family comprises buddies who share good spirits, occasions, holidays, and activities on a beautiful day.

Simple dinners shared become special because everyone takes part in preparing and cooking the meals. As you can see, the Blake family's way of celebrating occasions and even ordinary days is unique and fun-filled, yet not costly. They create activities and events they can share and enjoy together. Their bond is vital and profound because of it.

Chapter 5

LEADING

"If you can't see yourself serving, you shouldn't consider leading; leadership is service"

Your stepfamily is a team. But each member of the unit has their distinct personality, likes, and dislikes. For your team to function and thrive, you must consider the skills and attributes of each team member.

Managing your home is a daunting and challenging task that requires endless patience. When you become part of a blended family, you are entering an established unit. Your spouse's biological family, up to that point, has a set pattern of operation. As you merge your two families, you will adjust and share the leadership of your new unit. And the stepparent of the special child may find themselves on a steep learning curve.

Most of the time, since you want everyone to get along, you keep everything to yourself. But a leader needs to be heard and felt. You must address issues as they emerge. You are, after all, a co-leader. Your views make a difference, and your ability to lead your family is crucial. Below are five steps that will help you lead your blended family to success.

Building a Partnership

A united front. Committed. In sync. Consider these keywords and phrases as you go through your journey at the helm of a blended family. At the beginning of your union, you should talk to your partner about how you wish to deal with family matters (such as instilling discipline in your kids and making decisions for the entire family). That way, there is no room for laying blame when things do not go as planned.

The parent of the child with challenging behavior should take the lead as it relates to discipline, simply because they have a stronger bond and more experience relating to the child. However, that is not to say that the stepparent should always take a back seat. For example, a girl with special needs may gravitate to her stepmother and obey her even more than her biological father. In that case, it is acceptable for her stepmother to take the lead.

How can you have a good partnership? Like in companies and businesses where there is a common goal, families should have a shared commitment to building a solid and loving relationship for all members. Since yours is somewhat different from the typical family, you need to work twice as hard for your goals. And there is no need to worry—your difference can be used to your advantage. Being part of a blended family means you, your partner, or both of you have experienced previous partnerships. Apply previous lessons you've learned to your new family. As your family includes a special child, you have particular experiences that other families will not have.

You have undergone trials, made mistakes, and faced struggles. These are significant sources of learning. For example, if there were fights here and there about money in your previous marriage, then in retrospect, you can evaluate why money was a factor. This will help you avoid similar issues down the road.

Your blended family will only be as healthy and prosperous as your relationship as a couple. Even if you have previous experiences with difficulties, there will come a time when you face new and more challenging issues. Misunderstandings will arise. Problems will occur. As leaders of the family, you must be ready for them. Some of those problems may arise because of frustrations surrounding the care of your special child. It may be something as simple as getting the child to keep quiet or as challenging as allocating funds for their care. So, you must discuss and manage expectations early in the relationship.

Knowing early what you can expect from your partner and anticipating problems can help you both avoid unnecessary pain and misunderstanding. When you and your partner have established a solid foundation, committing to your family goals and aspirations is easier.

Making Decisions Together

Parents are leaders. In blended families with disabled children, parents need to make decisions to ensure that all the children get a fair deal so that the neurotypical children do not feel neglected. If this happens, jealousy can set in which can fester and damage the family structure. Open communication is essential for decision-making. It is best to be open and honest with your thoughts, feelings, and opinions, especially if it involves your children and stepchildren. When you consistently share your feelings, you generate trust. If there is a significant issue, have a meeting of minds to analyze the problem from different perspectives. Examine the pros and cons together to arrive at a more informed decision.

There should be honor and respect. When you discuss issues, allow each other ample time to talk. Listen intently and do not dominate the conversation. Keep an open mind. Never disagree right away until you hear all that is said. Listen to your partner and clarify if there are unclear and confusing ideas and suggestions. Do not let emotions get the better of you. Be rational and sound. When you are open-minded, you will think critically and rationally and be willing to consider alternative ideas and perspectives.

You and your partner can make joint decisions on some issues. However, the biological parent will occasionally have to take the lead. As the stepparent, you should know when to surrender and hand over the reins. This is often the case as it pertains to children with challenging behavior and disabilities. Once the decision is made, respect it.

There are other areas you need to consider when making decisions for your blended family. But open communication, honor and respect, and an open mind are crucial to achieving the best possible outcome. There are instances when you need the children's input when making decisions. If they are old and capable enough, do not hesitate to include them in matters that affect them. Your special child has a view, and even if he is non-verbal, you should get his opinions if your decision impacts him. If necessary, use visuals and offer choices. There is also the matter of your partner's ex. Never involve yourself when the issue is between them and is directly related to their shared children. Offer an opinion only when they seek your input.

Remember, you and your partner are the leaders of your household. Sometimes you'll have to lead; other times, you'll need to follow. That's why you need to communicate with your partner at all times openly. Otherwise, your team will not function well.

Your special child will genuinely test your leadership if they have behavioral issues. If these exist, you must do everything in your power to have the child assessed by an educational psychologist to ascertain how best to support their learning and development. Some parents resort to medicating when all else fails. That is a choice that you will need to discuss with health professionals.

Once you have the assessment from the educational psychologist, you can, based on his recommendations, decide on the best type of school (i.e., mainstream with support or a special school that focuses on teaching children with special needs). Be consistent—do not send mixed signals and interrupt routines in their day.

If your special child spends time with their absent parent, share the routines with that parent and ensure that both homes adhere to them and use the same approaches. If there is animosity between the ex-partners, do everything in your power to ensure that it does not sabotage your child's welfare. As adults, you must find common ground. The development and happiness of your child depend on it.

Instilling Discipline

Disciplining your children can be a complicated process. Every parent thinks about what can make their child happy and content. But there are times when you'll need to be firm, and that firmness may not make your child happy. You need to enforce stability and structure into a young person's life for their development. But what about disciplining your stepchild? It can be doubly hard because they may question your authority. They might think you're crossing the line and have no right to question their actions.

When your stepchild has a cognitive disability, they may not understand the discipline. For example, I wanted to punish my daughter one day, so I told her to go and sit in a corner. She didn't understand, so I led her to the place and asked her to sit there for five minutes. She turned the corner into a play area and found ways to play and enjoy herself there. My actions did not have the desired effect, and I had to abandon the idea of punishment. Now I take her aside and speak to her and ask her to repeat my instructions. I found this works better and has more lasting results even though she breaches our agreement from time to time.

You will need to discover what works for your child. This could be removing their favorite toy, removing their treats one week, or denying them a visit to their favorite mall. It is best to be led by the biological parent in this regard, especially if you are in the early days of your partnership. But whatever you decide, your kids need to see that you have a united front.

Don't undermine your partner's action by enabling their child to break the rules or override agreed sanctions. These can be subtle actions that, if left unchecked, can continue and grow into bad habits. For example, my daughter likes to reach onto another person's plate at the dining table and take whatever she wants. If I insist that she isn't allowed to do that and her dad proceeds to let her have food from his plate, what message would we be conveying to her? If this is not addressed early, she will repeat her actions in another environment.

Do's and Don'ts for Disciplining Children in Stepfamilies

Do's:

- Be patient
- Allow the child to speak and listen to what they have to say
- Discuss with your partner your methods for responsibilities, rewards, and sanctions
- Defer to the biological parent where necessary
- Support your partner in the actions taken
- Settle disagreements with your partner privately
- Openly discuss boundaries, values, behavioral expectations, and consequences
- Concentrate on building relationships with each member of your stepfamily
- Be empathetic.

Don'ts

- Don't change the rules unilaterally; if you have to change them, make time to explain why they have to change

- Don't experiment with your new stepfamily by trying to make up for past parental lapses or blunders
- Don't insist on discipline that is inconsistent with the style of the bio-parent
- Don't speak negatively about or undermine the efforts of the other birth parent
- Don't take it personally.

As a stepparent, you receive constant feedback and criticism. You may be subject to hostile remarks and rude attitudes. But what is your actual position in this process? I have already indicated that you should refer to the biological parent regarding consequences for inappropriate behavior. They should be the ones to handle the issue, but you must show support in the background. Your support will not only give your partner the needed help to follow through, but the child in question would also know that you are not someone he can recruit onto his side. The stepchild sees you as someone who goes by the rules. But at the same time, the child realizes you are not the enemy.

If you defer the discipline to your spouse, your relationship with your stepchild can grow. However, there are times when the bio-parent relinquishes their role of disciplinarian or asks for your help. This may be the case when the relationship between you and your stepchild is close enough that it becomes natural for you to impose discipline. When that happens, proceed with caution and love, but be firm.

In addition to being a stepparent in a blended family caring for a disabled child, I grew up in a blended family where a disabled child was part of the family unit. I now notice the happenings of my childhood being repeated in my adult life: parents often disagree on methods and severities of discipline. Parents sometimes discuss the matter privately, and then one takes the lead with the approval of the other parent who remains silent in the background. In the end, the discipline is not as severe as it could have been, but firmer than you expected. Essentially, they met somewhere in the middle. The following are some reminders in terms of discipline as it relates to your stepfamily:

- *Remember that you are a parent, not a peer* - Sometimes, you overlook this fact in a conscious effort to make your stepchildren like you. There's nothing wrong with having a friendly and casual relationship with your children, but there should be a fine line between being permissive and being too indulgent. Exert your authority so that they know to behave. They should know that you're the adult in the family. Never underestimate the ability of your special child to comprehend instructions and social cues. Their disability should not be at the forefront of your thoughts, focus instead on their ability and do not reduce your expectations.

- *Be Consistent* - You and your spouse should be on the same page when disciplining your children. If the rule is no video games on school nights, everyone must follow it. There should be no leeway or exceptions. Be firm with the agreed restrictions. Do not be swayed because your partner relents, and do not urge your partner to succumb to pressure. In the world of parenting disabled children, this is more difficult. Parents and stepparents often give in to their special child because of the consequences of not doing so. As a result, these children find it more difficult to regulate themselves, and they can exhibit very challenging and stressful behavior.

Consequently, we often just let the child have what they want. This is something that I cannot tell you how to handle. It depends on the dynamics of your family, how much you can take, and how your child behaves. But whatever you do, consider the impact on the other children and the long-term effect of your decision on your special child and on your family.

- *Be Fair* - The same rule applies whether you are dealing with a biological child or a stepchild. There should be no special treatment. They do not need additional conflict. Of course, when the child has a learning disability, you may need to adjust the severity of discipline. Still, it should never be that your special child gets away with unruly behavior while the other children watch in awe.

What is necessary here is that the other children are educated on the condition of their disabled sibling. It should be explained to them that the child is displaying behavior pertinent to his diagnosis, and for that reason, expectations differ. If they do not understand that, they will think it's unfair, which could lead to jealousy and resentment. Share information that you learned about the disability and let the children understand that their sibling is special but is not the only one with that condition.

- *Consult your partner* - Even if your partner gives you the authority in the matter, you should make it a point to ask for their input. And it would be best if you were transparent with them on what actions you are undertaking. This transparency will prevent them from questioning your decisions if things fall apart.

- *Do not overwhelm* - Do not impose too many rules and restrictions. Instead, give the children breathing space. Do not strive for perfection; it does not exist.

Working through Boundaries

One of the most complicated aspects of blended family parenting is disciplining the children. While allowing the biological parent to handle the enforcement, you can develop your relationship with your stepchildren. But do not be a pushover—set boundaries.

People often say, "Choose your battles." How true is this in a blended family setting? In any relationship, you establish physical and emotional boundaries. Physical boundaries involve your privacy, personal space, and body. Emotional boundaries enable you to separate what you are feeling from others. "Choosing your battles" might mean sacrificing your happiness for others and letting them dictate what you do and how you think.

Parents in a blended family environment must set boundaries with their children. And they must also impose limitations on themselves. Imposing rules and restrictions can aid both parties in their adjustment process. It can also lead to a fuller understanding of how to combine the two families' cultures effectively. You want to have a happy and well-functioning stepfamily, but as a stepparent, you do not want your stepchildren to walk all over you. To achieve the former and prevent the latter, you must understand the difference between healthy and unhealthy boundaries.

Some examples of healthy boundaries you can follow are:

- Respecting each other's privacy
- Placing value on your personal belongings
- Assigning specific chores at home
- Imposing a reasonable curfew when necessary.

Here are some examples of unhealthy boundaries:

- Taking out anger on one another
- Invading each other's private space
- Taking or borrowing possessions without permission
- Interrupting when one person is speaking.

When setting boundaries with your kids, you must have actual conversations with them. Speak calmly and rationally. Your children must not feel that you are imposing rules that are unduly harsh and stifling.

Setting boundaries helps ground the children's behavior and strengthens your relationship with them. Establishing structure can benefit the children as they grow up and empower them to function effectively in society. When rules and boundaries are laid out early, they allow for a smoother transition and adjustment process.

Flexibility is a necessary element in your stepfamily. You may need to get out of your comfort zone to obtain the best outcomes. Coming from diverse backgrounds, cultures, or upbringings, your stepchildren may not appreciate your boundaries, and you may have to adjust for a peaceful life. For example, your special stepchild may be accustomed to constant hugs and embraces. You, however, may not be comfortable with that. When you become a stepparent, you should be prepared to compromise. In this case, you could meet them halfway. After all, your leadership in this blended setting is essential because you are their guide.

So, how will you adjust your parenting style? Unlike your kids, whom you have guided since birth, your stepchildren were raised differently. For you to blend well, you must be the one to take the first step. In chapter 1 of this book, you read a discussion about cultural differences in blended families. As indicated, it is essential to understand cultural and racial differences. So, understanding their needs based on such a background is imperative if your stepchildren belong to a different culture or race.

Earlier in this chapter, we discussed discipline. When disciplining your stepchildren, you need to consider the kind of discipline they were exposed to. You do not want to shock them with a stern hand if they are not used to it or confuse them with a laissez-faire attitude if they're used to authoritative parenting.

Regarding studies and activities, some kids are used to being left pretty much on their own. If you suddenly start showing too much interest in what they do, they may feel overwhelmed. If you think that their existing habits are unworkable for your family, do not just impose what you think is right. It should still be the welfare of the kids you should consider. You will need to get out of your comfort zone by compromising and meeting your stepchildren halfway.

Here are some critical steps to take when attempting to compromise with the child:

- *Identify the core need of the child* – if you determine what is truly necessary for the child, it will help you discover the appropriate required action.

- *Consider the child's physical and emotional safety* – ensure that the selected course of action will not harm them.

- *Evaluate results* – analyze the outcome so you can check for an alternative action if the compromise is not working.

Chapter 5 explored the value of partnerships within the stepfamily dynamic. Be flexible in your approach. Decisions, boundaries, and discipline can all be achieved by being flexible and working towards a consensus where all family members thrive. Leadership does not mean power – it means leading the ship so that everyone plays their part for a safe arrival.

A Short Anecdote

Brian Birkbacher, a former football linebacker, responded when asked about his role model: "I love my mom, but my stepdad is my role model, the hardest working man I ever knew." Brian said that his stepfather is a true vision of exemplary work ethics.

What Brian said is very heartwarming. To be considered as your stepchild's role model is truly inspirational. To be seen as someone to be emulated is gratifying. To know that you are instrumental to your stepchild's success is overwhelming. The stepfather must have been so proud of his achievements and the love he had for him. It is easy to earn a child's love. But to gain the child's admiration and respect is something else. You can be a role model to your stepchildren by leading through example and leading with conviction and integrity. Doing so will significantly impact their lives. Just look at Brian's relationship with his stepfather, whom he lovingly calls "Dad."

Chapter 6

LETTING

"At some point in your life you have to let go of your baby"

Haim Ginott, a renowned psychotherapist and parent educator said "Treat a child as though he already is the person he's capable of becoming." Those are some wise words from someone who knows what his subject.

Sometimes, it's hard for parents to accept their child is growing up. Parents refuse to see their child is no longer the baby they brought home from the hospital all those years ago. The same can be said about stepparents. Loving stepparents want the best for their stepchildren, which sometimes results in overprotection and undermines the beautiful relationship you could develop with them. Allow your stepchildren to grow up and experience the world. Let them test the waters for themselves and develop their gifts for sharing with the world. Irrespective of any disability that your stepchild has, he has something to offer the world. Though he may need a higher level of protection, he must be given enough latitude to develop confidence and experience growth.

Children often accuse their parents of being overprotective. Parents say this constant vigilance over their children is due to several factors. But the most significant of these factors is *fear*. They fear that their children will make wrong choices and get hurt in the process. They fear the unknown and personal pain.

This fear drives parents to be strict with their children, sometimes to the point of suffocating them. It can create a rift that is hard to mend. If you want a happy stepfamily, your aim should be to build a solid foundation of love and trust with your stepchild. Avoid any possibility of a rift developing by addressing this unnecessary fear and allowing your child the freedom to explore and grow with the appropriate level of support.

Kids need freedom. When they have an appropriate level of independence, they can explore who they are. Stepparents must offer guidance, not chains. Allowing children to make their own choices within reason is beneficial for them and you.

As stepparents, we want the best for our kids. Most of the time, we believe that what is best for us is the right choice. But have you considered that what is right for you may not be suitable for someone else? To foster a great relationship with your children, allow them to make their own decisions (depending on their age and capacity to make decisions, of course). Children with learning difficulties, like neurotypical children, can learn to make their own choices. Still, every child needs some level of guidance. There are plenty of opportunities for you to allow your kids to choose, and in so doing, exercise their decision-making skills. Here are some of them:

What they Wear

What an individual wears allows them to express their personality. Typically, when parents decide what their children wear, their development in the style department is compromised. As soon as they are at the right age, allow them to express themselves. What is the right age? Professionals at the American Academy of Pediatrics believe that most kids learn to dress themselves by age three. This age may be somewhat early for some neurotypical children and especially early for children with disabilities. As a stepparent, you must be open to allowing your stepchild to have a say in what they wear, even if you are the one to select the possible choices.

Sometimes the child will make unsuitable choices. Instead of ordering them to change or being critical or condescending, talk with them rationally and let them understand why their option may not be appropriate. Do not crush their self-esteem.

Whom they can Befriend

Do not dictate to your stepchildren whom they should befriend unless you have valid reasons why they should not keep company with certain people. If you disapprove of their friends, explain why. No matter how much you think you know your children, you will never understand the feelings of enjoyment and comfort they have with certain people. If you are concerned that someone may be a bad influence, banishing that person from your child's life may have the opposite effect. Your child may even start lying to you about their interaction with that individual. A more effective way to handle this is to be a good influence and maintain an open, supportive relationship with your child.

What Books to Read

If a particular book catches your children's interest, encourage them to read it. Do not deprive them of the experience. It's funny to hear that some parents don't want their kids to read the Harry Potter books because of some "sensitive" issues.

American publishing expert Michael Norris states that despite their best intentions, "Parents have too much of a role in deciding which books their child will read" and "It is turning children off." You want your stepchild to read widely if they can read. If you are concerned with the content, talk about the material with them to share your thoughts and views. Children with learning difficulties may struggle in this regard, but many are passionate readers. If your child doesn't read, read to them. Never assume they're unable to understand.

Which Extracurricular Activities to Choose

Just because you love the theatre doesn't mean your kids will. And just because you're athletic doesn't mean they will be. Do not impose what you like on your kids. Let them discover what they enjoy and what they have a natural ability for. Encourage them in their choices, and you will see great results. When children are allowed to choose, they develop excellent decision-making skills. Making choices will help them in their future endeavors. And when you let your kids choose, you'll become a conduit to their independence. They'll love you for it.

Autonomy

According to Merriam-Webster Dictionary, autonomy means: "self-directing freedom and especially moral independence." Children typically express their desire for autonomy from when they are toddlers and into adolescence. Adolescents have a better understanding of the world they live in, so they want to partake in it on their terms. Even though your child has a disability, they still desire autonomy. They will likely observe what you do and then experiment.

At a certain age, your stepchildren desire independence. They may still be living with you, but they would like to lead their own lives. But while parents feel pride when their children become independent, there are times when they think it is too soon. When your child is disabled, you will be concerned about their independence.

Some special children will always need support, but that does not mean they should be denied an opportunity to be independent. It means you must assess the degree to which this independence can be granted. It could be that the child will never have the capacity to conduct his affairs and may need to live at home forever or in an environment where he receives care. Nevertheless, the child's need for independence must be considered and accommodated as far as possible.

Do not stand in their way when your neurotypical child wants to go to college in a different state. When the opportunity arises for your special child to go off to camp or other extended events, make it happen. You cannot wrap him up in cotton wool forever—the opportunity to be with others and away from you will work wonders for his confidence and learning. When you have a close relationship with your stepchildren, you know they will refer to you even when away. When you give them autonomy, you are reaping the benefits of your labor. They will feel that you value and respect their knowledge and capabilities.

How can you help them be autonomous? There are many layers: emotional, physical, and mental. You can do your part in making sure that your kids can transition to these different aspects. Following are some approaches:

- *Setting rules* - Remember the section in this book on working through boundaries? That's key here. While the idea is to grant autonomy, you do not want them falling through the cracks. By setting up rules to follow—such as curfews and dating restrictions—you are cautious while encouraging transparency and open communication. Without sounding too nosy, ask your children what they have been doing as casually as you can. Make it part of your dinner conversations and strengthen your bond with them with these daily chats. When your special child goes out for the day, greet him on his return and ask him how it went, even if he is non-verbal. Give him prompts. For example: "Where did you go? Did you go to the park? What did you see?"

- *Provide Growing Opportunities* - Within the family dynamics, you can give specific responsibilities and tasks to your kids. These responsibilities should go beyond just childish chores. Maybe it's as simple as deciding what the family has for dinner, what movies to watch when you go out to the cinema, or as challenging as planning your next family reunion. Let your special child help set the table for dinner, pour the drinks, or do other valuable chores that challenge them but they can do with a bit of effort. This action will let them know that you trust in their ability to handle significant family situations.

Take your children's freedom to the next level. Letting them be an "adult" from time to time has many benefits. It yields strength of character on their part, and you position yourself as their equal within certain situations. You are not just their stepmom or stepdad.

Space

Just like adults, children need and like their own space. That means being left alone to do their thing. In your desire to connect well with your stepchildren, you tend to overwhelm them with unnecessary fuss and attention. They don't need this, especially as they approach their teenage years or significant developmental stages in their lives. Experts say that kids today are less resilient, incapable of self-regulation, and unable to carry many responsibilities. You would think that they need further guidance because of all this. But no, according to these experts, our kids are this way because of *overparenting*.

Overparenting is when parents are excessive in their attempts to manage their kids' lives. While you might be allowing them to make decisions and have autonomy, you may still be hovering about incessantly. This hovering defeats the purpose of the first two areas of "Letting" that I explained earlier. Even if you only have the best intentions for your children, overparenting or micromanaging them could do more harm than good. Here are signs that you are micromanaging your kids:

1. Whenever they have friends over, you fuss about every little thing, such as what they eat or what they should do for fun. Leave them alone. You may be interrupting their fun.

2. You arbitrate without their invitation or permission if you hear that they've had small arguments with friends or siblings. This action results in a dispute between you and your child because they feel you are interfering.

3. You become too obsessive with the food they eat. In your desire to ensure that your children eat healthily, you control what they eat. Eventually, your relationship with them becomes unhealthy.

4. You find yourself eavesdropping on their conversations with others or checking emails and text messages. This action is going overboard with your parenting. Set boundaries for yourself.

Unless there is clear and imminent danger to their lives, you should stop micromanaging your children. A blended family is complicated enough without adding such drama to your relationship with your stepchildren. This can also happen when you micromanage your special child. Though this child may need supervision, you still need to allow them their space to develop their imagination and autonomy.

Part of giving your children space means allowing them to "live" outside their homes. Your stepchildren are now part of your family, having left their previous lives. You are now building a new home for them, but that does not mean they have left everything they had in their former lives. Whatever lifestyle they had before is still part of them, and despite your best efforts, they'll be living in two different worlds. You must respect that. Your stepchildren cannot be with you all the time. There will be birthday parties, weddings, and other gatherings from your side of the family that your stepchildren cannot attend because it may conflict with other events in their lives.

The early stage of your blended family is a time of adjustment. Apart from allowing them to have a life outside your home, you should provide the necessary support so they will not be overwhelmed with the back and forth between families.

Here are some of the things you can do to show your support:

- *Refrain from being resentful* - Recognize that it can be disappointing that they cannot be with you on special occasions, but there's nothing you can do about it. While building a new life with you, their connection with their first family should be sustained and nurtured. Situations occur in life, but birth families never change.

- *Encourage them to share stories about their birth family* - Let your stepchildren know you are interested in their lives outside your home. If they feel guilty about spending more time with one family than the other, you can alleviate their fears by showing them there is no competition.

- *Encourage them if you see that they are having troubles with their birth family* - If your stepchildren tell you that they are having issues with their birth family, help them work it out. Never make it a competition between the two families. Once that is settled, your kids will be thankful for your encouragement and assistance.

- *Avoid any conflict with the other family* - You do not need to be bosom buddies with your spouse's former in-laws. But it would be best if you kept a neutral stance with them for the children's sake. If difficulties surround your spouse's former partner, you must recognize that they will likely always be in your life if children are involved. Do not compete for the child's affection. Instead, refer any issues to the biological parent. If you see trouble between the absent biological parent and your stepchild, do not get involved and do not offer any negative opinions or comments. Keep the peace and be the supportive figure your stepchild needs.

Your stepchildren's social interactions with their birth family are significant. Do not deprive them of these essential factors in their lives.

Use of Technology

Younger generations are constantly glued to their handheld devices and other technology. It is not unusual for a child to receive the latest computer game on a birthday or other special occasion. Technology has infiltrated almost every aspect of our modern way of life. But when it comes to family issues, technology has its limits. The daily phone calls and texts are welcome; however, there is no substitute for face-to-face interaction. Experiences are better if they are shared in real life, not over screens. You'll know what the child is saying or feeling if you can look into their eyes. This is how strong family bonds develop.

While you might need to restrict time spent on gadgets, remember the age in which we live. Do not attempt to compare your childhood with your children's. It's a different era. Still, you must at least try to *limit* their amount of time with technology. Banning it at the dinner table, for example, is appropriate. Or if you are on a family outing, you can limit their time with screens then too. These are principles that must be communicated to the children early in your stepfamily journey. It is difficult to change when the horse is already through the gate.

When your child has special needs, you may be tempted to let them have their gadget for a bit longer if it calms them down. While that may be an effective strategy, you still need to control their use of screens slightly. A screen should not act as a substitute for human touch and attention.

Don't be *too* strict, though. Screens are an inevitable part of modern society, and you cannot afford to deny your children access and thus impede their integration into the community. Moreover, using smartphones and other gadgets is an important source of education and skill development—they will need them to socialize and for future employment opportunities.

Some children with special needs struggle to use a pencil but find it easy to manipulate a screen. Good knowledge of how gadgets work can also form a basis for a rewarding, enjoyable career. Most jobs require familiarity with computer systems, so completely denying your child access is not a smart move. Most issues around smartphone use can be addressed with effective communication. Emotional intelligence will enable you to find a balance that allows you to share quality time with your children.

Making Mistakes

You should allow your children to make mistakes here and there! Why? Aren't we supposed to *prevent* their mistakes, you ask? Not always. Allowing your children to make reasonable errors will be beneficial for them in the long run. Experience is a great teacher, and we acquire most of our knowledge and understanding through experience.

We do not learn how to drive by reading a bunch of driving dos and don'ts. We must get behind the steering wheel of life, and sometimes we make a wrong turn along the way. What's essential is that the driving instructor is there to offer guidance and minimize the risks. Our mistakes help shape who we are. Without them, there is no room for growth and development. Look back at your own mistakes from the past and consider how these have contributed to your development. How have these molded you into the person you are today?

Children eventually grow up. If you insist on engulfing them in a protective bubble because of fear that they'll get hurt, you may be setting them up for future pain and failure. Many families mistakenly believe that their special child will never understand danger, so they never expose them to situations where they may get hurt.

Of course, you should never put your child in harm's way or let them make a mistake that can cause severe damage. But if you see your child attempting to take a small risk and you know that the outcome is not ideal, measure the risk with the learning opportunity. For example, I allow my daughter to pour our drinks even though I know she will spill the drinks or may even drop the container. I balance that learning opportunity with preparation by ensuring that when she spills the drinks, there is a catchment like a tray, and if it falls on the floor, I have the materials ready to clean the area.

Consider the benefits of allowing your children to make mistakes:

- *Self-Confidence* - People develop self-confidence after experiencing and overcoming an issue. Mistakes enabled people to learn and appreciate what they needed to progress in life. Your children will not be confident just from your words of encouragement. No matter how wise, beautiful, or talented they are, they will learn more from personal experience. Sometimes they will fall face down. They may even cry for a while. But the day will come when they start to smile again and are more equipped for the future. Let them gain self-confidence by not being afraid of making mistakes.

- *Responsibility* - Responsible people are made, not born. We become this way because of the roles we are assigned. So how do mistakes make us responsible individuals? They don't. Owning up to our mistakes does. When your kids own up to their mistakes, it is not an admission of failure or defeat. Instead, it is a reinforcement that they can assess their actions and find ways of improving. They become responsible individuals. Accepting both the positive and negative outcomes of their choices is essential. It strengthens their character and motivates them to do better next time.

- *Wisdom* - Aren't wise people wise because they know what they're doing? No, that's not entirely true. Intelligent people make mistakes. They become smart because they forgive themselves, learned from their mistakes, and continued. Wisdom is a trait that we do not typically associate with youngsters. And that is a problem. Your children cannot rely on you all the time to make wise and intelligent decisions, so allow them to problem-solve. Learning from their mistakes will enable them to gain wisdom and knowledge.

Overparenting your special child prevents him from becoming wise and responsible as he grows older. Sometimes, stepparents are guilty of trying too hard, which results in kids becoming annoyed and irritated. Let them have the space they need as individuals. If they are a danger to themselves and others, step in when necessary. If your child has mobility issues, that does not mean you must avoid moving. If that child can walk, it may be worth letting him take the steps with the necessary support.

If their other birth parent is in a relationship, recognize that your stepchildren are part of two blended families. These kids need all the support and understanding you can give them. Accept the fact that you cannot have your stepchildren all to yourself. Your children need to grow and develop on their own. Do not be afraid of letting them make mistakes—they are integral to making them stronger and wiser.

Remember, children do not exist in this world to remain as kids. Even if they are severely disabled, they should not be under your wing all the time. Let them fulfill their roles in your home, the community, and the world. Allow them to grow and lead their own lives.

Chapter 6 explained that your children are not just your children; they have their own lives to lead, with or without disability. So let them face the world and all its scary obstacles. Doing so will allow them to grow into the kind of person of whom you can be proud. Self-confidence, responsibility, and wisdom are all excellent traits to have in our changing world. Enabling them to develop these skills is the best gift you can give.

A Short Anecdote

Helen, an actress, and spoken word artist talks about her stepmother Valerie in an interview. She recounts how Valerie was instrumental in her development from a challenging teenager with dyslexia to a successful adult. Valerie entered her life when Helen was 12. Valerie is a mother to three sons and treated Helen as a daughter. Valerie included Helen in family matters and gave her responsibility as a big sister to her younger siblings.

The responsibility Valerie gave Helen allowed her to grow into an independent individual. For that, she is genuinely thankful. To Helen, Valerie was not just a stepmother but a trusting friend who came into her life at a critical moment after she lost her biological mother. She explained that Helen allowed her to make her own choices while still asserted authority at the right moments. According to Helen, Valerie was protective of her but was always objective. She treated Helen as an equal, respected her wants and needs, and allowed her to become a strong-minded individual.

One day, you can be like Valerie with a stepchild like Helen, who will have nothing but sweet praise for the way you raised her in your wonderful, blended family.

Chapter 7

LIFTING

*"Strength is not shown in putting, pushing or pulling down;
it is demonstrated in putting, pushing and pulling up"*

Families are complicated, and blended families can be even more so. Relationships are often formed under challenging situations. For your family to brave these complexities, you need to lift each other. No one should be left behind. Everyone should grow as the relationship progresses.

A blended family faces additional struggles and challenges compared to typical families: extended families, adoption issues, custody battles, and more. To stay afloat, the family must inspire, motivate, and help one another. We live in a fast-paced world where it's difficult for families to spend time together. But try to remember that quality is always better than quantity. Even though you cannot always be physically together, you should still make your presence felt. That can be as simple as sending a text message to see how one is doing or as elaborate as giving a gift. These moments are crucial because they convey to each family member that they are dear to you and that you are there for them no matter the situation.

Past occurrences may have caused people to feel wary and unsure of one another. Some kids who experienced abandonment or abuse are constantly worried about what could happen in a new environment. So, you must work to eliminate all these negative thoughts and feelings. You need to establish a bond and strengthen that bond within the family. You must always be there for each other to ensure a happy and content environment.

Encouragement and Praise

"You can do this!" "Hang in there!" "Never give up!" "Stay strong!" These are some of the most well-known encouraging phrases that lift our spirits. Whenever we are down, hearing such comforting words from the people we love makes us stand up quickly from a fall and face our problem head-on. No matter how loving your home is, stepchildren will likely carry emotional baggage. Some of them recover quickly from the pain of their original family's breakup; others don't. Some children will always grieve over a parent's death. Adopted kids generally have abandonment issues. We must make our children feel we are with them throughout their coping struggles.

Kid problems seem trivial compared to ours. But they are immensely challenging. Working on an assignment or reviewing for an exam can be tricky, and fighting with a best friend is emotionally draining. So put yourself in their shoes. Encourage them to work out their difficulties, and they'll know that they always have a shoulder to lean on.

Words of encouragement like, "Bravo!" "Good job!" "You were amazing!" "Thumbs up!" uplift and strengthen us. They give us a sense of happiness and fulfillment. After encouraging your children with a task or a problem, compliment them for a job well done. Appreciating them in this way nurtures their sense of self. They feel like they have accomplished something worthwhile. Children with challenging behavior enjoy these sentiments. You will see their moods uplifted.

Talking about the accomplishments of your child makes them happy. Never miss an opportunity to praise their efforts and success, no matter how big or small. Express how proud you are of them so they can feel good about what they have achieved. A person who is praised by others feels worthy. An employee who is complimented by a superior feels valued. A child praised by a parent becomes joyful. Praise is one of the most powerful gifts a stepparent can give a child.

Encouragement and praise work hand in hand. If your kids are apprehensive over an upcoming examination, provide them the motivation they need to do well. And if they do a good job, give them a pat on their back for a job well done. After giving them inspiring words before a major competition, do not forget to enlighten their spirits by commending them for their skill and effort. When you encourage and praise your children, you are practicing positive parenting. No matter how big or small the endeavor or achievement, your encouraging words mean a lot to children.

Now, with all this support and encouragement that you offer, you might be forgetting yourself. Lift yourself up too. Explore new hobbies, attend classes, do anything that makes you feel good. Support and motivate yourself, so you have enough positive energy to share with others.

Expressions of Love

They say action speaks louder than words. Maybe, but not always. Sometimes, we need verbal expressions of love and affection to be uplifted. Expressions of love are essential—not just to your biological children but also to your stepchildren. Since your relationship with them can be considered raw and fragile, your actions of love may be lost amidst all the complexities. Let them know that you care for them with your words.

This goes beyond kids. Let your partner know how much you love them. Stepparents are very concerned about building relationships with their stepchildren. The result is they tend to forget why they have stepchildren in the first place—through their marriage or relationship. You might think your partner already knows you love them, and that may be true. But they may still be in a vulnerable position because of what happened in their previous relationship. You cannot afford to neglect or take them for granted. Express your love to them as much as you do with your children.

Why is it important to express our love? Regardless of age, sex, or status, all of us need love and affection. Nothing beats being told you are loved and appreciated by people close to you.

- *Expressing your love reduces whatever pain and hurt a person is feeling* - When your partner, child, or stepchild feels sad and lonely, telling them they are loved will lift their spirits. The feel-good phenomenon appears when you hear "I love you" because of the release of oxytocin (what experts call the "love hormone"). Try it when your child is having a tantrum, and then watch him calm down. Whisper to your partner these precious words whenever they have problems at work, and he is sure to bounce back. Then he will reciprocate, making you feel good too.

- *Expressing your love makes the recipient more confident* - Hearing loving words makes us feel important. That feeling of importance makes a person confident. When your children or stepchildren feel down in the dumps, afraid, or unsure of themselves, tell them how much they mean to you. This assurance will turn everything around for them.

- *Expressing your love makes other people feel safe and secure* - knowing that you love them increases your children's feelings of security. They are assured that they can always count on you for help. Your spouse and stepchildren may be feeling vulnerable and anxious as they enter this blended family with you. Tell them you love and care for them so these feelings can be placed on the back burner.

- *Expressing your love decreases stress levels* - This goes both ways. If you or your partner feel stressed and tired, hearing beautiful words of love will calm them. If your partner comes home from a grueling day at work, express your love and lift his mood. If your children had a rough day at school, express your affection for them. These words of love will energize them quickly. And when they tell you that they love you back, any stress and anxiety you feel will diminish or disappear.

Some people think being expressive of feelings is corny and outdated. These beliefs are baseless. Nothing beats hearing that you are loved and cared for. Telling each member of your family that you love them conveys appreciation, support, and trust. Don't be afraid to tell your partner and children how much they mean to you. Saying "I love you" is easy and meaningful. Tell your spouse, your biological kids, and your stepchildren how much they all mean to you. Lift your family with love.

Finding Opportunities for Growth

In any family, all individuals need growth opportunities. As heads of the stepfamily, stepparents must find ways for each of their children to grow and develop. And they must provide an equal share of opportunities for both their biological children and stepchildren. This can be anything from after-school activities to hobbies to club memberships. When your kids express a desire to participate in those activities, you should encourage them to enhance their skills and talents.

There are many advantages to allowing your kids to have such opportunities. They will enhance their skills, hone their talents, and build confidence. Find activities that are relevant to your special child. If there are no groups in your area, you can establish one for parents of children with similar disabilities. These activities can be an additional element to your child's "Life Outside of Home." The groups can become support for you.

If funding is an issue, be open and honest with the family about your affordability. Whatever you do, be fair. Make sure everyone has equal opportunities. If you have neurotypical children in your stepfamily, ensure they receive their fair share. No one should feel left out or unimportant. If necessary, you can also make compromises and allocate time to the kids' activities and performances.

The important thing is you maintain equal opportunities for everyone. There'll always be fights and jealousies within the family, especially for a blended one like yours. Just try your best to maintain a loving and fun atmosphere in your family.

Making Learning Fun

It's not easy building a happy and harmonious blended family. Fights, misunderstandings, and struggles will arise. But you will do everything in your power to make it work.

So, how can you counteract conflicts and disagreements? The answer is family fun—a crucial part of building a solid family identity. When you create a fun family environment, you ensure a lifetime of happiness and contentment with each other.

You should also strive to enhance the minds of your children. Keep them on their toes with continuous learning at home. Although they're attending school, a child's learning and education should start at home. Parents are the primary teachers of children; they should maintain a good home/school education balance. However, your children should not feel that your home is a full-on extension of school. Make learning at home fun! Implement exciting activities and reward them for good behavior, progress, and excellence. Here are some actions you can take at home that can result in a fun learning experience for you and your kids:

- *Play a learning game* - Play educational games with your kids. This could be as basic as alphabet blocks or something more challenging like word vocabulary or science board games. You'll not only help them become more intelligent, but you'll also playfully connect with them. Tailor the game to facilitate your special child, too. You must never assume that he cannot participate.

- *Watch a movie* - You can watch an educational show, a documentary, or even an average movie. Then, you can talk about it with your kids when it's done. This activity will help enhance their comprehension level. And hey, you'll have fun watching! When you are working with your special child, you may want to stop the film intermittently to talk about what is happening.

- *Make craft items* - Making craft items at home will nurture their creative minds and be fun for all parties involved. Use rudimentary items and recyclable articles to explore the creativity of the child.

- *Play sports* - Your kids who are into sports can practice their skills at home. If space and finances allow, you can set up a basketball court or other amenities where the family can play. You can play with them or just watch to support and encourage them. And you can always go to the local park if you don't have space at home.

There are other fun things you can do with your kids at home. Make your blended home somewhere they can look back on as a space filled with fun and joyous moments.

Inspiring to Aspire

You might feel like you have to protect your special stepchild all the time, but you need to let them find out who they are. Even if your child has impaired cognitive capacity, they are individuals with their own minds, desires, and aspirations. Take every opportunity to nurture them so they can proceed on their path to self-discovery. So, how can you inspire your stepchildren to be the best version of themselves?

- *Research* - Being a parent is a lifelong learning journey. That means you may have to conduct research. Before, people relied on instinct and intuition when it came to parenting. But in this changing world, there are sources of information that can help you empower your child so they have the best chances.

- *Observation* - Spend time observing your kids and discovering their innate talents and skills. Doing so will allow you to find appropriate activities for them to hone their skills and abilities.

- *Encouragement* - Encourage your child to follow their dreams. Please do not assume that because they have disabilities, they have no goals. Once you observe and see what they like, feed that talent with words and acts of encouragement.

- *Practical support* - Be a constant source of support as they embark on their paths into adulthood. That means you have to help with application forms for jobs and school, follow-ups, and sourcing of opportunities. No matter how old your children get, and even if they insist they can do everything independently, they will always need you. Help them become the best they can be.

They say blended families are complicated. And while that may be true, they can be a lot of fun too! Chapter 7 shows that you can manage complexities with a fun and enjoyable blended family experience. The key to achieving this is to encourage, support and inspire every member of your stepfamily to grow and thrive, leaving no one behind.

A Short Anecdote

Meet Hayley and Jeff. They are parents to three boys and three girls who are all adults now. When they were married, the kids' ages ranged from 5 to 10. In an online interview, Hayley was asked what she thinks was the best part of belonging to a blended family. She said it was all the fun they had together. They did have their share of ups and downs, but she and her husband made it a point to integrate fun and laughter into the family dynamic.

When things got busy, they used their dinner conversations to talk about what was going on in everyone's lives. These talks paved the way for them to reach out to their kids if they needed encouragement or support. Hayley said, "Our initial goal was also to make sure the kids knew they were loved, wanted, and cared for. It was hard, but I am happy to say that our family eventually took shape."

Stories like Hayley and Jeff's are impressive. Continue to uplift the members of your family to have the same success they had.

Chapter 8

LUBRICATING

"Life has its ups and downs but no one has to be down for another to be up"

As you build a blended family, expect friction to occur. Your stepchild may not be receptive to your constant attention, or your biological kids and stepchildren might not get along. You and your partner may argue, and you may find yourself taking sides with the children.

Although these issues sometimes escalate to the point of frustration, there are many ways to address them. And sometimes it comes from the most unexpected places. To guide your family to a place of joy, you need to engage in additional activities that "lubricate" the bond within the entire family. If your stepchild exhibits particularly challenging behavior, it can be a burden on your family.

My neighbor has a child who displays challenging behavior and consistently hits his stepsiblings. She adopted the strategy of taking the child for long walks, which she says makes him exhausted and calmer on his return home. Different situations call for different measures, and targeted action steps tailored to the situation can help eliminate friction or hostility within the family unit. When the steps taken are effective, they promote inclusion and cohesion that help strengthen the family dynamic. They also help your family achieve a peaceful and happy environment, which will get you through challenging times.

Maximizing Family Time

Time waits for no one. In our attempt to keep up with life, we often ignore or forget the best things in life. Manage your time wisely so you can have the opportunity to lubricate your family.

Spending time with your family is crucial. Your kids become adults in the blink of an eye. You need to cherish each moment with them and build lasting memories. These moments and memories do not just apply to big occasions like your kids' graduations or birthdays. Dinner chats and movie nights are some of the small activities that can strengthen family bonds. Find time, and you'll find happiness and contentment.

So, how can you find time in this busy world? If we can find it for shopping trips and nights with friends, we can devote time to family. The following are some strategies to ensure that family activities can occur more frequently.

- *Create regular family time* - When you've established activities, it will be easy to find the time to slot them into your routine. Discuss this with your husband and children so that you can come up with a consensus on when your family time will take place. It would be best if you had family time every week.

- *Take advantage of unplanned days/times off* - When storms occur, schools tend to close. Or maybe you get off from work early. These are some of the instances you can use to your advantage. While cooped up inside, come up with an activity that you can do together. Do not make the excuse that you need to "catch up on sleep."

- *Sit down together for a meal* - Make mealtimes more of a social gathering than simply a time to fill your bellies. Dinner chats are where families typically build strong bonds because they can be both intimate and relaxing—just pure talk of what happened during the day. Conversations help establish real connections.

And don't forget date nights with your partner! You should not neglect the core relationship of your family. While you must spend more time with your kids, you should not ignore your partner. Have fun with them often, whenever your schedules allow for it. Strengthen your bond so it can carry over to the rest of the family.

Creating Rules

Parents usually create the rules. But when kids get a bit older, they should be involved. Since these rules mainly apply to them, they must have a say. To strengthen the foundation of your family dynamic, involve your children. Some decisions in the family need to be taken up with them. Their views and suggestions about rules must be taken into consideration. Make them feel valued and essential. If your child is non-verbal, use cards, sign language, or any other method of communication they can use. Give them choices and continue to speak to your child, even if you think they do not understand.

It's best to collaborate with the entire stepfamily when creating rules. This way, there will be very little room for complaints as everyone will feel accountable. They are less likely to break the rules if they make the rules.

When setting rules, you must discuss the kind of consequences that would apply. For younger kids, explain to them what the rules are. And for older kids, involve them in the process. It does not work the same way for children with special needs. There will be no room for excuses on their part if they do break them. They should not escape punishment if that is part of the deal. These children often do not understand the relevance of rules, and though they may understand consequences, they are still more likely to break the rules.

When they are part of the process, they will have a better sense of responsibility and follow the rules more. On the other hand, it will be hard for them to break the constraints that they built. They know that rules are founded on fairness.

There's another benefit in allowing your children to help make up the rules: they become more aware of their accountability. They cannot disregard or question regulations they helped build. They become responsible for enforcing them. You might not notice it, but involving them in the process develops their critical thinking skills and helps them look at different situations from different angles. They'll need these skills for future endeavors.

When you collaborate with each family member to create rules, cooperation and trust will grow. This collaboration will add to the strong bond you are working so hard to achieve. Consider the children's input. Don't just make them air out their views, then disregard them. Show them that their opinions matter and are relevant.

Allowing Independence

Adding to value and importance, allow your children the autonomy and independence they need. Help them become self-sufficient early. No age is too young for children to start standing on their own two feet. Even children with disabilities can learn independence, though they may still need to be monitored. They should make contributions to the family. Encouraging them to be independent will only lead to a great future as sufficient members of the community.

Earlier in our "Letting" chapter, you discovered the importance of autonomy in a blended family. This aspect is also integral in "Lubricating" because allowing your children to be independent and self-sufficient can bring two benefits: strength of character and harmony within the family. Having independence means a lot to your children, especially the older ones. It makes them feel competent and like they can hold their own. You can reinforce those feelings by being supportive when they make decisions for themselves.

You can also provide them with the necessary tools for self-governance. For example, they can learn how to go shopping and manage their finances. You can also consider putting them in charge of something essential and elaborate, like planning a birthday party. This responsibility would help them think and act solely at their discretion. Just be prepared to provide backup and support for your special child in this regard.

How can you lubricate your stepfamily so your younger stepchildren can benefit? You might not think that they will be able to participate, but there are several ways wherein younger children can have a taste of independence:

- *Let them make their snacks* - Making snacks is something they can easily do without your help. And they will enjoy the outcome! Just ask them to whip something up from the fridge, then let them get creative!

- *Let them complete specific chores* - What kinds of chores? You can assign someone to set the table. Then, another child should clean up after dinner. If a child has a specific task that they are responsible for, they'll take pride in it. They will do their best not to mess up. Each child will be extra careful and diligent in doing the specific tasks assigned. Children with special needs can play a part in this quite easily, too. Focus on what they can do and let them do it. Do not be afraid to stretch them a little beyond their comfort zone. Take every opportunity to teach them. Specific duties and chores make children keener on doing well. And since they feel responsible for the given assignment, they will try to complete it to the best of their ability.

- *Ask for their opinions or ideas* - Children love to be treated like adults. Ask their opinion on the gift to get for their dad's birthday, what movie to watch, or what meal to prepare for dinner. Doing so will mean a lot to them and make them feel grown-up.

Encouraging your kids to fend for themselves in various situations can help enhance their sense of self. Doing so also allows you to polish the structure of your family and allows for independence.

Offering Rewards

"The reward for work well done is the opportunity to do more." - Jonas Salk.

Typically, when a person is rewarded for good behavior, they will repeat that behavior. That's why most parents reward their kids for something they did well. And you can use these incentives as a means for your other children to follow suit. For example, if one child sees that their sibling is rewarded for picking up her toy, she will most likely do the same. They will engage in the same kind of behavior because of their desire to be rewarded.

Your special child may or may not follow the example, but as a stepparent, you must continue to model the desired behavior. In your blended family, remember to maintain equality. You may have labels—biological kids, adopted kids—but they are all your kids now. Treat them the same in all aspects, including when to reward them.

What types of rewards am I referring to? It depends on the situation, but they can be either material or social. Material rewards are extrinsic and could be anything from toys to chocolates. Don't go overboard, though, and align the prize with the accomplishment!

Social rewards are intrinsic, non-material things such as praise. Words like "You did great!" or "Way to go!" This reward can come in the form of affection: a hug, a kiss, or even a pat on the back. It can also be an extra privilege, like permission to go to bed later. Rewarding your children has pros and cons, and it ultimately leads to positive outcomes like:

- *It makes children feel appreciated* - Whether you reward your kids for a small accomplishment (such as finishing their chore) or something huge (such as winning a competition in school), they feel your appreciation. This recognition makes them feel good because they know their time and effort did not go unnoticed.

- *It makes them feel special* - It feels good to be singled out for excellence. When a child is told "Good job!" for cleaning his room, he feels special and is more encouraged to clean his room again. If you add a reward to reinforce the feeling, the cleaning of the room becomes a habit.

- *It can raise their self-esteem* - When receiving a reward, children feel privileged. And with that comes self-esteem. So, build up your kids' confidence by recognizing them for something good they did.

- *It can improve your connection with them* - Children appreciate and value you more if you give them rewards. You become instrumental to their happiness. And although the bonus lasts only a short while, your connection will last longer.

By rewarding your children for good behavior or tasks accomplished, you create a more pleasant atmosphere in your home. Do not deny your kids incentives. Rewards and surprises keep your children happy. Provide enjoyment for your family by engaging in rewarding activities.

Sometimes, families get stuck in old routines: breakfast, school, lunch, homework, dinner, and bedtime. Life can get boring for kids and adults. Sometimes you need to break the monotony by boosting the feel-good factor in your stepfamily.

There are many different strategies you can use to break monotonous routines. One would be to introduce pleasant surprises the entire family enjoys. Research indicates that a good surprise brings vitality into our lives. Some experts say that being surprised helps us gain focus so that our attention is directed to looking at a situation on many different levels. It is essential in making our minds and bodies deal with stress better.

Why must we surprise our kids? There are many reasons, but some of the more important benefits are listed below:

- *It stimulates their minds* - When you surprise your kids, it lets them know you will try new things. Whatever you surprise them with will add flavor to their lives. They feel excited, and they become more alert and energized. As a result, their cognition improves.

- *It takes their minds off problems* - Even for a little while, kids can forget whatever problems they have in school or elsewhere in life. Also, if there are any existing conflicts between stepsiblings, surprising them with something meaningful and fun can divert their attention.

- *It gives them (and the parents) a chance to build lasting memories* - Whatever the surprise is, it's an opportunity for all of you to make new memories to cherish as a blended family. You will look back and reminisce about how happy and content your family is because of these fun events. They can be conversation pieces for years to come.

How can we pleasantly surprise our kids? There are many ways aside from the usual out-of-town trips or new clothes and toys. You do not need to spend a lot of money. Here are some creative and inexpensive ways to add fun to a routine:

- *Camp out in your backyard or the middle of your living room* - Camping will surely add flavor to your kids' lives—and yours too! Think of all the fun you'll have while imagining that you are all surrounded by nature.

- *Have a picnic* - A picnic is a sure winner. They never fail to integrate fun into our lives. And you can soak up some sun!

- *Go to a local amusement park* - Going to an amusement park is always fun for kids and adults alike. Games, rides, funnel cakes—who wouldn't love it?

- *Adopt a puppy/kitten* - Unless there are health concerns, you can surprise your kids with a new pet. A cute puppy or kitten can always brighten up our kids' lives.

- *Pick your kids up from school early and go out for ice cream* - Apart from the joy that kids will feel because they are getting off from school early, the idea of going out for ice cream will excite them. No school and ice cream = a great combination!

- *Have a sleepover in your bedroom* - Cuddling them in your bed and telling them night stories are good ways to end the day. They will feel closer to you.

The list goes on. Your family does not need to be rich to experience these kinds of surprising and joyful activities. But you will be richer in love and affection.

Some children with learning difficulties also display challenging behavior that some families find difficult to manage in public. And so, because of fear, these families often avoid taking the child into public spaces. While I recognize that it can be stressful, I believe it is unfortunate and harmful to the child. Stepfamilies with special children must understand that they are an integral part of their family unit and deserve to interact with others in public spaces. This is how they learn, grow, and appreciate how society functions.

It is also essential for them to be seen by other people who may have an unhealthy impression of disabled children. Therefore, the family, and society in general, stand to benefit by embracing these children who are themselves gifts, bearing gifts. As parents, it is your role to ensure that the gifts they are bearing are given to the world, for a gift is not a gift until it's given.

Chapter 8 is all about strengthening the bond of your family. When you create and implement rules, spend quality time with your family, or give rewards and surprises, you lubricate the wheels of your stepfamily so that it can move smoothly and sustainably and thereby promote peace and joy in our blended family.

A Short Anecdote

Nell has been married to her husband for 22 years. They formed a blended family with four children. The children were all under the age of six when the family blended. Then, their son was born a few years later.

In the early years, the kids were constantly bickering and fighting for attention. They came up with a plan: they started going on dates. But not with each other—with their kids! They took turns taking out the boys and the girls. The children got to decide what they would be doing and where they would be going, and it worked wonders for them. Not only did the parents and kids have fun with the activities chosen, the "dates" also put a stop to the fight for attention.

Spending quality time with their children in this manner eliminated relationship issues in Nell's stepfamily. And she and her husband grew closer than ever. All it took was a proper amount of trust, persistence, and creative thinking to bring peace to the family unit.

Chapter 9

LEARNING

*"When life ends learning ends; when learning ends life ends.
Life without learning is not living"*

As long as we live, we learn, even if we don't want to because life itself is a great teacher. As the parent and caregiver of a special child, you are responsible for creating and identifying opportunities for your family to learn. Everyone in your family unit should learn about the disability of your special child and understand how it manifests. Research the condition and keep abreast of developments in the area. These actions will enable you to be more informed and thus engage more meaningfully with official personnel and respond more effectively to people who may be curious. In addition, although the conditions are lifelong in most cases, from time to time, treatments and therapies emerge that may benefit the child or young adult.

At this point, I want to take the opportunity to share some resources that I developed and used with my daughter to help build her vocabulary, enhance her reading and numeracy. The Pocket Learner educational development system is a relatively novel, flexible, multi-award-winning invention developed precisely for those reasons. It is used by both neurotypical children and those with learning difficulties. If your special child has difficulty grasping those concepts, the Pocket Learner is a tried and tested resource that the entire stepfamily can use. Further details can be found online.

Every blended family goes through trials and tribulations that might leave you wondering, "Is this worth it?" Sometimes, you wonder what others are going through. You ask yourself, "Do other parents have challenging stepchildren?" or "Do they feel as exhausted and conflicted as I do?" and even "Do they have family disagreements regarding how to raise their kids?"

Being a parent or a stepparent of a child with cognitive disabilities can be the most rewarding role. But there are moments when you may feel defeated, and envy other families you think are having an easier time. In movies, stepmothers are depicted as evil women who make their stepchildren suffer. It can become overwhelming at times, and you may occasionally feel like bursting into tears of anger and frustration. You may have friends to console and support you, but it's difficult to express your feelings or seek advice from someone without a similar experience.

Just know this: you *are not* alone in your journey to achieve a happy stepfamily while caring for a child with special needs. There are thousands of parents going through the same situation and asking the same questions you are. When going through a rough patch, do not despair. Seek out stories from other families. Be inspired by their experiences.

Books and magazines are helpful, but they cannot beat the real thing. First-hand experiences and personal testimonies will help guide you.

Learn from other men and women who have traveled your path. Observe how they transformed their family from one of distrust to one of love. Find out how a vulnerable and unsure group of strangers turned into a happy and devoted family.

Some of the following stories were not as successful, but you can learn from their mistakes. These stories will fill you with the inspiration and motivation you need to keep going. I encourage you to make a conscious effort to learn from these incredible journeys.

Story No. 1: One Step at a Time

According to Catherine, having kids was never an intention for her when she was younger. So, it is pretty ironic that she now finds herself with two biological children and three stepchildren, one of whom has special needs.

Catherine said her current scenario was something she would never have imagined. Her blended family was fraught with difficulties regarding accommodation, awkward adjustments, jealousy, gender rivalries, and resentments. She and her husband put a lot of thought into physical space. They asked the step-siblings to share rooms along gender lines, thinking this was an excellent way to bond. Harry's disabled son Mark shared a room with Catherine's son. These children did not get ample opportunity to bond before they all moved in together. Catherine and Harry had dated for only six months, and although their respective children knew their new stepparent, they had met their new siblings only once on a family outing.

This idea was a disaster. The conflict surrounding Catherine's daughter and her two stepdaughters escalated so fiercely that they had to abandon the concept after only two weeks. Looking back, Catherine and Harry acknowledge that it was a mistake to use space as a means for the children to bond.

Sometimes your gut tells you it is not a good strategy, says Catherine. There were signs that the arrangement would not work, but they ignored them and "hoped for the best." But that "hope" was at the expense of the children, especially her daughter, who felt betrayed. Her son Jaycee seemed to tolerate Mark, and that's all it was.

Catherine's Advice to Others Starting a Blended Family

Take it slow. Blending a family takes time and effort. There is nothing automatic about it. You need to let the children get to know each other before moving in. The idea of thrusting strangers together in a room is not a good one, even if they are children.

Prepare your children for the change. Help them to manage their fears about the new arrangement. Do not decide without consulting them about something as important as living space. Consider your children's thoughts and feelings before deciding on matters of the family. Do not rush them into something for which they are not ready. Let them spend time with each other before the move and iron out any conflicts in this early phase. Forcing your children to bond with your stepchildren by sharing space is too much to ask and in most cases, will backfire. Take everything one step at a time.

For some families, circumstances such as finance, religion, or geography may make it necessary to move in together quickly. However, if you can do it gradually, that's a better way to go. Moving your children into another home arrangement in steps makes it easier for the children to adjust. You could also try taking your children for an overnight stay at the new home now and then so that they can get used to the new space while still having their own home. It can give you an idea of how the new living arrangement will work so that you and your partner can make adjustments before the complete move takes place.

By making the children part of the process, they can feel part of the decision-making rather than simply being something happening to them. This can make a massive difference to the success or failure of moving in together. Sit down and talk to your children about the fact that the move is going to happen. Listen to and address their concerns. They may not have a choice in the matter. But, let's say they are kept informed as the relationship develops rather than told when everything is already settled. In that case, they are much more likely to feel valued and convinced that their needs and emotions are considered.

Story No. 2: Regrets

With all the difficulties that come into forming a blended family, one might ask, "Are there any regrets?"

When Penelope met her husband David, he already had children with several different mothers. So, she enters into a large family of stepsiblings and adds her kids into the mix. According to Penelope, two of the kids have challenging behavior. It turned out that her 13-year-old stepson was diagnosed with Attention Deficit Hyperactive Disorder (ADHD) and her 9-year-old stepdaughter has autism. She had no experience with children with special needs - this was uncharted territory for her. Nevertheless, Penny did her best to ensure that the family did not fall apart.

So, to answer the question - No. Penelope does not have any regrets. On the contrary, the experience made her a stronger person. She realized that by building her stepfamily on a foundation of love she was able to see the child and not just the behavior. She enrolled in autism awareness courses and joined a group for parents of children with special educational needs and disabilities. She shared what she learned with the older children, who are adjusting their expectations and reactions and now helping their siblings perform some simple tasks. Penny's home is still somewhat chaotic, but she said she wouldn't trade it for anything.

Penny's Advice to Others Starting a Blended Family

Being a stepparent can be difficult; you have to be prepared to adjust in all areas. You may have to change your traditions, enroll in classes, learn new skills, and manage your expectations. Join an online parents community where you can interact with people who understand the issues - ask questions, get answers and share your triumphs and challenges. A disabled child brings added burdens, but when you get it right, it is the most rewarding. This journey is not for everyone; test the waters before diving in!

In order to establish a successful relationship with your stepchildren, you will need to be clear on your role as a stepparent before combining families. When disabled children are involved, you must be clear on how their disabilities affect their behavior and what will be expected of you as it relates to their care.

Some people with learning disability have more than one diagnosis. You will need to understand that you will be both a stepparent and a caregiver. If you are unwilling to take on that role, you may want to reconsider whether this blended family is for you.

Story No. 3: Double Whammy

"Our life is chaos." That is how Gloria and her 16-year-old daughter Minnie describe their life as a blended family. Gloria has three children from a previous marriage and two stepkids. Minnie is the eldest of the biological brood. Two years ago, Gloria was diagnosed with an incurable illness that makes her tire easily and impedes her mobility. So, apart from looking after her siblings, Minnie has responsibility for taking care of her stepsiblings, one of whom has profound and multiple learning disabilities (PMLD). He receives a few hours of support per week, but the family has to care for him at other times. Gloria feels guilty about the pressure she places on Minnie, causing her to miss out on her teenage years.

Minnie willingly helps her Mother, but she yearns for change. She finds herself a caregiver at a young age, and though her stepdad is a good-natured man, he works long hours and is hardly around to help in the home. Minnie's schoolwork is beginning to suffer and she is often late for school. The family is stressed out.

Gloria's Advice to Other Stepparents

Things can go wrong in your stepfamily, but that's not reason enough to give up. Your children can be a big help, and the experience can make your family even closer. While your elder children and stepchildren can step in to help the younger ones, do not put pressure on them. If possible, enlist outside help or support from the extended family. Do not take your children for granted; remember to thank them for their support, listen to their concerns and make sure they know they can count on you even if you are in poor health. Tell them how much you appreciate their help and understanding; praise them for their efforts.

The situation in Gloria's family occurred through no fault of hers. Life happens, and unfortunately, even in typical families, things can take a turn for the worse, and sometimes it breaks up the family. Her disabled stepchild is entitled to support and is already known to the Social Services Department. In cases like these, do not hesitate to contact them to access any further help available. In addition, some countries have a department that supports families in need, and some organizations provide grants for a range of items for disabled people. Conduct an online search for these organizations, and do not be afraid to ask other parents for information.

In a blended family, the children are the most vulnerable and thus are most affected when things go wrong. Therefore, take every opportunity to access any external support that is available for your family.

Story No. 4: Stepping into Her Shoes

Dianne is a stepdaughter who found herself at the other end of the spectrum. At the age of 19, she became a stepmother herself. According to Dianne, her stepmother entered her life when she was very young - the only memory of a family was the blended one when her stepmother married her father. She had always looked up to her stepmother, but never in her wildest dreams did she imagine that she would become one herself.

Dianne became a stepmother to Sam's three-year-old daughter Suzie at 19. Sam had just ended a stormy marriage and acrimonious divorce and had gained sole custody of Suzie. His ex-wife was not allowed to see Suzie until she could prove that she was fit for the purpose. She was, therefore, very bitter and disrespectful to Dianne. In addition, Suzie had just been diagnosed with autism, and at the age of three, she was still non-verbal.

Suzie was not handling the breakup well, she was having behavioral issues, and Dianne found herself in unfamiliar territory, despite her experience of growing up in a blended family. Suzie turned four, and Dianne realized that she had to go to school, and as a child with special needs, there were several procedures to be completed for her to access the right level of support.

Stepping into her stepmother's shoes was not easy, but she stayed the course just like her stepmother did. Despite the rocky start, Dianne describes it as the most rewarding choice she has ever made. She joined the parents' group and found new friends. In addition, she has enrolled in a course that will give her a new career in special educational needs.

Being a part of her stepdaughter's formative years has been a blessing.

Diana's Advice to Other Stepparents

Whether you are new to this game or not, challenges will abound. Irrespective of whether you grew up in a blended family or had one before, you will still encounter new experiences, for no two families are the same. Experience helps, but you will still be tested. When a child with special needs is added to the mix, there are other dynamics to consider. It is a different world, and you have to learn quickly. Your patience will be tested but instead of looking at their stepchildren as reasons why they should give up, look at them as to why they should dig in. Hang on to that love to see you through.

Diane thought it would be a walk in the park, that she had it under control. You may think you are ready to take on the challenge, and you may, but never assume there'd be no challenge because you've seen it all. But, as Dianne integrated herself into her husband Sam's family, she knew that she had entered a different world.

Story No. 5: Unique Family

Most of the stories we hear are from stepmothers. Rarely do we hear any testimonies from stepfathers. Typically, when it comes to the nitty-gritty of stepparenting, we only look at how mothers are faring. But dads, too, have to adjust, and they often find themselves at a loss as to what to do. So Tom's story may interest you.

Tom and his wife are not stepparents . Their blended family is unique as it comprises four children: two biological sons, an adopted daughter who has cerebral palsy, and a foster daughter. And just like other kinds of blended families, this one has its share of issues. Tom had this to say about being part of his family: "It is incredible, innervating, embarrassing, pride-giving, life-giving, depressing and uplifting." Only in blended families can you find such a diverse and interesting choice of words. He said that his family has contact with their adoptive child's origin family, which extends their already complicated and unique dynamic. But that's what makes their lives rewarding.

As he sees his daughter thrive in their home, knowing that he had a hand in making her comfortable and content was a blessing. The way the entire family has become attached to her is pretty unique too. When Tom saw the new birth certificate to make his daughter's adoption legal, he could not help but marvel at their family's situation. Sure, their family is not typical compared to other families, but the happiness and contentment are quite the same.

Tom's Advice to Other Stepparents

Whatever kind of family you have, whether you conceived the child or not, the peace and joy you feel inside are unique. No words can describe all the emotions you feel. Embrace that feeling. Embrace your extraordinary experiences being in a blended family.

There are different types of blended families. Tom's family is atypical but falls within the remit of a blended family. His adopted child has cerebral palsy, which is not classified as a learning disability, but some people with cerebral palsy might have a learning disability. Tom does not say whether his daughter has a learning disability, but it makes no difference, and his family unit is a happy and healthy one based on his comments.

Story No. 6: Wake-up Call

"No one wants to be in this family." That's what Emma's husband kept telling her. She felt annoyed and angry with him for uttering such words. To her, he was just not trying hard enough.

However, as the days wore on, Emma saw the cold, ugly truth of what Ken was saying. Emma's 14-year-old son Junior refused to listen to anything Ken said, and he ignored Emma's guidance. He refused to be in a room with his stepdad and consistently stayed out later than he should. Emma's other child, Gillian has Fragile X Syndrome with a mild learning disability. She refused to speak to anyone and spent inordinate amounts of time in her room.

Communication in the stepfamily was practically non-existent. Sheer frustration prompted the couple to reassess their situation. Sensing that they were at breaking point, Emma and Ken stayed up late one night to talk about their family and whether it was worth staying together. Individually they had blamed the children, but when working together, they concluded the following:

- Their children didn't choose their situation. Instead, they were thrust into a situation they did not want, and they didn't have time to bond with Fred before he moved in with them
- The idea of a blended family reduces the attention each child gets

- Seeing Emma and Ken together is an emotional trigger for the children. It angered the two children who felt that Fred had dislocated their father. They didn't seem to care about the emotional abuse their mother suffered.

Emma and Ken worked out a plan whereby Emma would dedicate 15 hours of one-on-one time with each child every week. They spent that time on various activities inside and outside the home, and occasionally, she took both siblings together. She used this time to improve the communication between the three of them and show them why their father had to go. In time Fred joined the trio but ensured that he deferred all matters of discipline to Emma.

Ken's Advice to Other Stepparents

Though you love your partner and want to spend time with them, you must take stepparenting slowly. The children will resent you if they feel you are the reason their family broke up, even if you had nothing to do with it. Go easy with the children; if you assert yourself as their dad, they will resent you, and when that happens, you can have no joy. Do not try to change them; just be patient and love them.

Emma and Ken also realized that they were unprepared for what it takes to be a stepfamily. But most parents of blended families are unprepared because they underestimate the dynamics. While they have the experience from first families, it is not the same with blended ones. Even with all the effort, their kids can still be uncomfortable and angry and have divided loyalties. So keep working on your stepfamily. Use the principles of 9 Ls in this book to help you through.

Story No. 7: A Steep Learning Curve

Anne is a 46-year-old woman who is going through her second divorce. She has regrets. She regrets the day she met Mark and his 9-year-old son Ted to whom she refers as a spoiled brat. Ted had consistently hit Anne, and she had lashed out after two years of maintaining her calm. Ted has a diagnosis of Attention Deficit Hyperactivity Disorder, and Anne is convinced that his behavior drove a wedge between her and Mark.

Ted told his mother that Anne had hit him, and that was the beginning of the end. Now Anne is out of the picture, spending time thinking about how things could have been different. However, she insists that her expressions of regret have nothing to do with her marriage to Mark. Instead, she regrets all the stress, hurt, and complexities that emerged. Some painful words were expressed, awful behavior displayed, and inappropriate actions on all sides. To Anne, those are the aspects that fill her with remorse and sadness when she looks back. She had no warnings; now, she realized that she was unprepared for the role of caring for a child with special needs and thus was surprised by the dysfunction that came with a blended family.

Anne's Advice to Others Starting a Blended Family

If your stepchild has special needs, make sure you understand how it affects them before agreeing to enter their family. Get some training and spend time getting to know the child before making a decision.

As in typical families, some blended families do not succeed. Even with the best precautions, things can fall apart. If they do and you decide to leave the stepfamily, do not bear grudges. Recognize instead that it did not work out this time. And painful as it may be, avoid blaming anyone, pick up the pieces and continue to live your life to the best of your ability.

Story No. 8: Blood Isn't Always Thicker

Fred helped bring up his stepson Ron who had Asperger's, after he and Ron's mother divorced. Ron was about seven years old when his mom and Fred married. Ron was 13 when they separated, and he continued to live with Fred until his adult life. He maintained a good relationship with his mother and his birth family, but no one understood him as well as Fred.

Fred's Advice to Other Stepparents

I took Ron on as my own, and now that his mom is no longer a part of my life does not mean that Ron ceases to be mine. On the contrary, once you show love to your stepchild, he will reflect it to you. When the bond is well established, blood is not thicker.

Fred is one of the many stepdads who recognize that parents and stepparents separate or divorce; however, they don't divorce their children or stepchildren. Instead, they continuously love them and look after them. Stepfamilies face countless challenges, but all these can be resolved if everyone will unite and cooperate.

Story No. 9: Life Lessons

One thing that benefits parents in a blended family is an attitude of continuous learning. Each day brings about a new lesson for stepparents in their journey to achieving a happy stepfamily.

The last testimony is from Cindy, a 46-year-old woman who states that her stepfamily is unique, unlike any other family she knows. When Cindy met her ex-husband Brian, they were both in college, and he already had a 9-month-old daughter called Briana. Cindy cared for Briana when it was Brian's turn to keep her. After their marriage, Brian gained full custody of Briana, and they became a happy stepfamily.

When Briana was 11, Cindy gave birth to a daughter called Camilla. She had to make adjustments so that her stepdaughter would not be affected. After all, she had been the center of attention for more than a decade. Cindy had to relearn everything to care for Camilla, who was later diagnosed with global developmental delay. Cindy says Brian could not cope with Camilla's disability, and the marriage broke down. They divorced when Camilla was five years old. Briana, now almost 17, chose to continue living with Cindy and Camilla as they had developed a strong, loving bond. She helps her stepmom care for her young sister, who is becoming a very responsible and caring young woman.

Now, after four years of being single, Cindy is embarking on a new journey with Johanna, the mother of a girl with Down's syndrome, whom she met at a group for parents of children with special needs. It's new territory for her and the children, so she is taking it slowly. The children are getting to know Johanna and her daughter, but there is no plan to move in together anytime soon. Nevertheless, Cindy is conscious of the lessons she learned in her previous relationship and is making sure that her new relationship does not adversely affect her family unit.

Cindy's Advice to Other Stepparents

Having a disabled child in your stepfamily can put undue pressure on your relationship. The demands of the disabled child make it difficult for you to allocate equal time to your spouse and your other children. You have to bring them all along with you, and what I mean by that is you have to make them part of the process. Though you may have less time for them, make the time you have with them memorable. In addition, encourage them to be involved in caring for the disabled sibling but never force them to do so.

When embarking on a new relationship, take it slow. The children in a close family unit may start to feel neglected if they think that you have suddenly started to focus on a stranger. Your new partner must get to know the children and spend time with them before any moving in together can take place. Do not ignore the signals from your children. Listen to their concerns and help them through the transition. Remind them that they are loved, and their opinions matter.

Some parents and stepparents find it overwhelming to have a child with special needs in the family unit. These children need more care and support in areas such as mobility, personal care, and communication. As a parent, you can help your child by enabling them to build on their strengths and getting the proper support to help them overcome the activities they find difficult. Every child is unique, but with the appropriate level of support, children with learning disabilities will lead fulfilling and rewarding lives.

How we Learn from the Stories of Other Stepparents

Let these stories inspire you on your journey as a stepparent. When we read or hear another family's story, we make connections with our own reality. We can then find answers to questions we may have about stepfamily life. After all, humans have communicated and connected since the beginning of time by telling stories.

The stories presented above may or may not apply to your stepfamily, but each one discusses elements that may surface in your journey as a stepparent. The accounts show joy, pain, uncertainty, and the successes and failures some encounter along the path to a happy stepfamily.

Chapter 9 demonstrates that stepparents can learn from the stories and experiences of other stepfamilies. Doing so will allow them to see reflections of themselves and feel more aligned and encouraged, knowing that their experiences are not unique to them. In summary, stepparents can understand their situations better when they hear how other families address similar circumstances.

CONCLUSION

Whether you are a stepparent, sibling, stepsibling, or a member of some other non-conventional blended family, you will appreciate that finding balance and harmony despite the distinctive dynamics in your family is not always easy. However, now that you have reached the end of this book, you can understand that this goal is achievable. And when you are successful, you will realize that there is something magical and profound about being in a stepfamily.

Since every family member has a unique personality, thinking style, and set of beliefs, it is unreasonable to expect a merging family to hit it off straight away. Stepsiblings may take a while to adjust to the new family structure.

Several factors can adversely impact the early success of the stepfamily - the development of new relationships, variations in parenting styles, discipline, and interpersonal conflict. Partners may also struggle in their new roles in the stepfamily.

Like a typical family, a blended family caring for a disabled child experiences successes, failures, challenges, and uncertainty.

Once you have laid the foundation in your launching phase and built the appropriate structure, you will experience more ups than downs. Build a blended family based on love and laughter. Doing so will empower you to face the challenges head-on irrespective of how difficult they may be. Listen and respect everyone in your blended family, even if you think they cannot communicate or understand. This is particularly key to the development of your special child. Actively listen to each other and maintain open and frequent communication.

When a disabled child is part of a stepfamily, the family will function differently. These children can bring added challenges, but they can bring just as much added joy. They have their part to play, and when this is acknowledged and facilitated, the potential to grow and learn, and the resulting chances of success, are multiplied. Everyone can learn and contribute, so when stepfamilies raise their expectations and encourage participation and inclusion, they build a cohesive family unit permeated by love, laughter, joy, and peace.

Give your special child the same respect you give to others by including them in decision-making. Let them have the appropriate levels of freedom to thrive. Let your stepchildren have the chance to express themselves through their words and actions, guided by your leadership. Lead your family towards the path of collaborative decision-making, boundaries, discipline, and routine. And while you lead, allow your children to experience freedom and independence. Avoid over-parenting. Be the rock that supports your stepchildren during times of struggle.

Take time to lift everyone in your stepfamily, including yourself and your partner, with encouragement, praise, and inspiration. Of course, stepparents must instill discipline, but they must also try to maintain a happy home. When they go the extra mile to create time to spend together, involve the children in higher-level decision-making, and give them responsibility, they elevate their stepfamily to another status. They build a stepfamily that can weather storms—one in which a disabled child thrives and can take on our world with a confident heart and head.

Your commitment—not just to your spouse but to the entire family—is integral to a happy home. Lubricate your blended family by lavishing encouragement, praise, fun, and expressions of love. Don't forget the little things. Sometimes, trivial matters are what can keep you going.

Having learned the nine Ls, get out there and create a loving, inspiring, and healthy family you know is within your capability!

RESOURCES

1. A story of a blended family - ReachOut Parents. (n.d.). ReachOut. Retrieved May 31, 2021, from *https://parents.au.reachout.com/common-concerns/everyday-issues/things-to-try-blended-families/a-story-of-a-blended-family*
2. Applebury, Gabrielle. Blended Family Problems.
3. https://family.lovetoknow.com/fun-family-outdoor-activities
4. Basic Special Education Acronyms & Glossary of Terms
5. https://abbreviations.yourdictionary.com/articles/acronyms-for-special-education.html
6. Blended family Frappe
7. A handy guide to those mysterious blended family acronyms!
8. https://blendedfamilyfrappe.com/blended-family-acronym-guide
9. Bright Horizons Education Team. (2019, August 12).Benefits of Nature for Kids. *https://www.brighthorizons.com/family-resources/children-and-nature.*
10. Cascade Health. (2016, November 4). Self-Care for Stepparents | Cascade Health. Cascade Health | Cascade Health. https://cascadehealth.org/self-care-for-stepparents/

11. Chapman, K. (2019, August 5). This Is The Cold, Hard Truth About Blended Families. Scary Mommy. https://www.scarymommy.com/blended-family-truth/

12. Chertoff, J. (2018, December 19). How to Navigate Challenges as a Blended Family. Healthline. https://www.healthline.com/health/parenting/blended-family-tips#honor-differences

13. Davies, I. (2021, May 20). 60 Touching And Inspirational Stepmom Quotes To Show Your Love. Find Your Mom Tribe. https://findyourmomtribe.com/stepmom-quotes/

14. Givens, Aisha. (2019, July 16). Blended Families Can Work. Youth First Blog. https://youthfirstinc.org/blending-families/

15. GoodTherapy Editor Team. (2020, August 4). Blended Family Issues. Blended Family Issues. https://www.goodtherapy.org/learn-about-therapy/issues/blended-family-issues

16. Holloway, S. (2021, March 25). How to Deal With Money Problems in a Blended Family. ToughNickel. https://toughnickel.com/personal-finance/How-to-Deal-with-Money-Problems-in-a-Blended-Family-Stepfamily-Money-Issues-Financial

17. Koo, B. (2021, May 25). 61: Guaranteeing a Return on Your Investments. Wealthy Mom MD. https://wealthymommd.com/blended-families-need-know/

18. Kumar, Kalyan. ©2017 Nifty Journals. The Benefits of Socialization for Kids. http://niftyjournals.com/2017/07/benefits-socialization-kids/

19. Liles, Marilyn. (2020, January 9). 101 Quotes People in Blended Families Will Truly Understand. https://parade.com/977564/marynliles/blended-family-quotes/

20. Lynn, C. (2019, August 12). Blended families-a story of survival - Cheryl Lynn. Medium.

20. https://medium.com/@lynneletterio/blended-families-a-story-of-survival-7bf9228730c0
21. Randy White. © 2004 White Hutchinson Leisure & Learning Group. Interaction with Nature During the Middle Years. https://www.whitehutchinson.com/children/articles/nature.shtml
22. Robinson, L. (2021, April 20). Blended Family and Stepparenting Tips. HelpGuide.Org. https://www.helpguide.org/articles/parenting-family/stepparenting-blended-families.htm
23. Schwartz, Allan. Empathy vs. Blame
24. https://www.mentalhelp.net/blogs/empathy-vs-blame/
25. Shrayber, M. (2019, June 5). If you come from a blended family, these real-life accounts will hit home. Upworthy. *https://www.upworthy.com/if-you-come-from-a-blended-family-these-real-life-accounts-will-hit-home*
26. Social Security Administration. Disability Benefits
27. https://www.ssa.gov/benefits/disability/
28. Souders, B. M. (2021, April 6). Parenting Children with Positive Reinforcement (Examples + Charts). PositivePsychology.Com. https://positivepsychology.com/parenting-positive-reinforcement/
29. The first two years in your blended family. (2019, April 11).
30. Raising Children Network. https://raisingchildren.net.au/grown-ups/family-diversity/blended-families-stepfamilies
31. Virella, L. (2018, March 18). Do you regret marrying into a blended family situation? - Quora [Comment on the article "Do you regret marrying into a blended family situation?"]. Quora. https://www.quora.com/Do-you-regret-marrying-into-a-blended-family-situation

32. Waldbieser, J. (2020, October 28). Our Blended Family: What I've Learned as a Single Stepparent. Healthline. https://www.healthline.com/health/parenting/my-blended-family

BLENDED FAMILY

A Guide for Stepparents

Seven Unsuspecting Attitudes
That Are Seriously Toxic to Stepfamilies

Andrea Campbell

Pocket Learner Publishing

PREFACE

There are certain dynamics to consider and process when two families join. Getting used to the role of stepparent can be stressful and adjustment takes time. Combining two families under one roof can prove challenging; even for the most prepared, there will be periods of discomfort and pain in the process.

Children are affected when their original family breaks up and a blended family is formed. They find themselves having to adjust to a new parent and new rules. They may express their frustration with this process through behavioral or emotional outbursts. Children may struggle with feelings about a new stepparent and feel unloved or feel as if they do not fit. These dynamics affect the new stepfamily. Stepparents will find themselves having to balance emotions with duty.

When you consider the presence of other parties, such as birth families, grandparents, former partners and family friends, you find that a range of factors can infiltrate the home and cause added stress and uncertainty to the family unit. When faced with this mish-mash of factors, stepparents often make the error of tightening the reins in hopes of reducing or eliminating outside influence and restoring order to their home.

Overparenting is when parents are excessive in their attempts to manage their kids' lives. While you might be allowing them to make decisions and have autonomy, you may still be hovering about incessantly. Even if you have only the best intentions for your children, overparenting or micromanaging them will likely do more harm than good. Here are signs that you are micromanaging your kids:

1. Whenever they have friends over, you fuss about every little thing, such as what they eat, what they're wearing or what they should do for fun. Leave them alone. You may be interrupting their fun.

2. You arbitrate without their invitation or permission if you hear that they've had small arguments with friends or siblings. This action results in a dispute between you and your child because they feel that you are interfering.

3. You become too obsessive about the food they eat. In your desire to ensure that your children eat healthily, you control what they eat. Eventually, your relationship with them becomes unhealthy.

4. You find yourself eavesdropping on their conversations with others or checking emails and text messages. This action is going overboard with your parenting—set boundaries for yourself.

Unless there is a clear and imminent danger to their lives, you should stop micromanaging your children. A blended family is complicated enough without adding such drama to your relationship with your stepchildren. This can also happen when you micromanage your special child.

Though this child may need supervision, you still need to allow them their space to develop their imagination and autonomy.

I have written this book to show that there is another way. Fighting fire with fire is never a good idea; it is always better to grab a bucket of water, even if it's against everything you believe. Ultimately, your home is where you should feel most secure. To achieve this, you must take steps to promote peace in your stepfamily.

INTRODUCTION

Blended families are often the result of a breakdown of the original family or the death of a parent. It is understandable, therefore, that children experience intense and sometimes overwhelming feelings of anger, disappointment, and sadness. Some experience grief, guilt, and anxiety, leading to depression and feelings of insecurity. When a parent remarries or moves in with a new partner, children face further threats to their sense of security and stability.

Some seventy-five to eighty per cent of divorced parents in the USA remarry. This means that many people face the need to adjust to this significant transition.

Every parent of a blended family aspires for their child and new partner to get along. If the partner also has children, the new couple will hope the children bond quickly so that the new family can settle down and function normally. It takes time for a blended family to stabilize, and it can be upsetting when there is misery in the household despite the adults' best attempts to make things work. Sometimes, in despair, parents make mistakes in the approaches they adopt to achieve cohesion and happiness in their new family unit. Unfortunately, the failure to address issues, or the hope that they will simply disappear on their own, rarely yields positive results. If they don't get the dynamics right, parents will struggle to maintain a happy and healthy household. In many cases, they fail and become yet another statistic of unsuccessful blended families.

I wrote this book to help stepfamilies navigate this challenging but potentially enriching role. A successful blended family takes more than the desire or intent to make it work. Stepparents must adopt and apply a range of skills to keep their families together while maintaining flexibility. The seven elements presented in this book are often overlooked or are lost in the noise of contemporary society, where parents are busy juggling the different facets of their lives. However, if you pay attention to the elements I have outlined, the difference will be noticeable, and your family will be on its way to finding peace.

I've dedicated my professional life to supporting parents of children with special needs from varying backgrounds. Having grown up in a blended family, and now being the mom and stepmom of a family with a special child, I have seen how this unique family type, also referred to as a stepfamily, can produce happy, resilient, and confident children with or without special needs.

I have also seen how quickly things can go wrong. This is often because of unconscious attitudes which can become embedded and adversely impact the stepfamily. Attention to these seemingly minor issues can make a world of difference in any family.

Working with families from different cultures has enriched my outlook on blended family life. I have had opportunities to live and work in several countries, and I have learned that one size does not fit all. There's no single winning formula for building a happy blended family, especially when that family is caring for a differently-abled child.

Blending families can be a complicated and challenging transition to navigate. The observations I have made throughout years of professional work with families and personal experience contribute to the information I have presented in this book. This non-traditional checklist outlines critical factors that, when routinely overlooked and unchecked, can damage families and deny them the peaceful existence they desire and deserve. I hope to encourage personal introspection and reflection, followed by concerted action to initiate and consolidate change. Stepparents should discuss the factors with each other in honest conversations to explore how they could improve their experience, starting with small sustainable steps that benefit each family member.

The seven attitudes I present spell the word BLUNDER because, in my mind, that is precisely what stepparents do when they adopt these attitudes or fail to address them.

This is a concise text for the parental figure needing a quick read. I want to draw your attention to my full-length book, "Blended and Special", available wherever books are sold. The in-depth book is a compilation of strategies for issues confronting blended families as they navigate their way in the world of stepparenting children with special needs.

Also available is the book: "The Pocket Learner–Special Needs Education," which presents a unique framework to empower families of children with special needs to support their children's cognitive and physical development. This book is a comprehensive guide to caring for children with special needs from the very early years up until adulthood.

I hope you find the material in this book insightful. So let's dive right in!

Chapter 1

BUREAUCRACY

"You can do a good thing but it may not be the right thing"

Rules are essential in every sphere of life. We live by rules, many of which we implement ourselves and gladly follow. For example, you can't just approach someone in the street and hug them. This is an extreme example, but is it universal? Why don't we do it? Where is the rule written down that prohibits this sort of behavior? It is written nowhere, and yet we abide by it! Adults in a family unit often establish and implement strict orders and rules, which weigh down the family, causing undue stress and misery. This sort of bureaucracy is damaging to families. Insisting on officialdom, procedures, and strict rules creates unnecessary stress in your stepfamily.

All families have rules–spoken or unspoken. However, rules are generally more noticeable in stepfamilies because, as two families merge, they combine their traditions, routines, and habits.

Early in the union, there must be discussions between the parents about the rules in your home as you raise your children. These may differ based on the home culture where the child lived before the stepfamily was formed. For example, a child raised in a particular religion may want to attend religious events, which may not apply to the other children. Notwithstanding the existence of rules and levels of authority in the household, a stepparent should be primarily a friend or confidant, not a disciplinarian. Biological parents should remain primarily responsible for discipline until a solid bond and trust have been well-established.

Rules and Differently-abled Children

Children with special needs, especially when they have cognitive disabilities, often do not follow the rules. Stepparents must find creative ways to introduce the rules to these children to aid their learning and encourage them to establish appropriate behavior. For example, my daughter had the poor habit of taking food from the plate of others while sitting at the dining-room table. She did not consider this to be unacceptable. As a family, we consistently discouraged this behavior and did not yield to her desires. Soon enough, she learned she had to focus on the food on her plate instead of other people's. As is the case in the neuro-typical child, teaching children with special needs is a constant undertaking.

A child with special needs who is non-verbal requires additional latitude as they may not be able to articulate their feelings, including any pain or illness they may be experiencing. While you want them to conform and treat them like any other child, you must remember that they are living with a disability and, in some cases, may have complex needs. These circumstances demand extra patience and understanding.

Adaptability in Blended Families

Even as your family works to establish consistent expectations, some rules may have to be broken for the sake of peace. If a child capable of making his bed doesn't do it one day, it is not the end of the world. Let it slide if he doesn't want to eat with the family today. Yes, we want all these social rules to be followed, but what will happen if they aren't? Would you prefer a child who flaunts the rules from time to time or a child who decides to run away or turn to strangers for what they see as a loving environment? The child will eventually yield to your instructions as they feel respected, loved, and understood. They must not be bombarded with strict rules. That is not to say they will become perfect; it only means they will work with you more often. Little by little, both sides will make concessions to achieve greater peace in your household. Slackening some rules also reduces stress and helps you save energy for critical issues.

An adaptable stepfamily will change as circumstances evolve. Though each family member may have set tasks, there needs to be a measure of flexibility that will not destabilize the family if any member falls out of line. While parents must maintain structure, they should avoid being autocratic or emotionally abusive.

Homes with excessive bureaucracy often have a clinical look, with a specific place and time for everything. Mealtimes are at the same time every day, and the menus may be set for different days. The children may be required to eat in silence unless their parents invite them to speak. These families may pride themselves on maintaining structure and instilling good manners in their children. In those situations, the children do not feel free to share information such as the day's events or any concerns they may have, and the stepfamily misses out on chances to bond. Worse, they may miss out on opportunities to save their children from making unnecessary and costly mistakes. The lines of communication must remain open to access the information you need to keep your children safe and address emerging issues early.

When stepparents maintain a household with exceedingly rigid rules, they risk becoming distant, imposing figures, and children may seek closeness or affection from any available adult. These circumstances put them at risk to abuse as they turn to people outside the family unit for what they see as love.

Notwithstanding the suggestion to avoid being overly strict with the children in your stepfamily, it is important not to swing too far to the other extreme where families become chaotic. Peace doesn't thrive in chaos. In chaotic families, there are few rules, or existing rules may change at a whim based on the parents' mood. Also, unacceptable behavior may warrant punishment at one moment and not the next. There is no set place for objects in these households, and family members can eat when and where they like.

While some people may think they are happy in chaos, that is not the case for most. The desired position is somewhere in-between a highly bureaucratic approach and chaos. Together with their children, stepparents must find the right balance that works for their family unit.

Imperfect Stepparents

Stepparents often experience guilt due to the failure of previous relationships. There is no reason to feel guilty if you gave it your best. Families, irrespective of their makeup, are not perfect. If you think you failed in your former relationship, see this new relationship as an opportunity to get it right. Don't dampen the environment in your home by being too rigid. Instead, strive for joy in your family unit. Believe you can succeed even if the way forward is unclear.

Parents in traditional family structures don't have perfect lives, irrespective of what outside appearances might suggest. Parenting is hard–whether biological or stepkids. When one or more children are differently abled, there are even more demands on the family. Try to go with the flow sometimes, and do your best. If you're honest with yourself and your partner, you'll put the children's needs first and let go of perfect. You'll get there in the end.

Don't pressure yourself, your partner, or the children to live up to an ideal you created or to which you aspire. For example, if your stepkids don't want to call you Mom or Dad, don't take it personally. I understand that you may feel hurt since you are playing the role of a parent, but at the end of the day, you are not their biological parent and therefore being acknowledged as Mom or Dad might never happen. That's the reality, be at peace with it.

Key points
- Some children find it challenging to follow the rules, and it is up to stepparents to be creative and flexible.
- Order is essential, but avoid overkill if you wish to reduce or eliminate stress in your stepfamily.
- Prioritize peace and joy over rules and order in your stepfamily.

Chapter 2

LAMBASTING

"Learn to ignore the subject but pass the course"

Closely linked to strictly enforced rules in the home is the issue of discipline. This subject is essential in bringing up children to function effectively in society. It is, therefore, not about the *what*; instead, it is about *how* children are corrected, taught, and trained. But, again, this is not an either-or situation; there is a need to balance both.

Children with special needs, too, must be subjected to discipline. Do not assume that the child will not understand or assimilate instructions because they have a disability.

In my earlier example of my daughter dipping into the plates of others around the table, most parents would be quick to rebuke their neurotypical children but perhaps not their child with special needs. Both children must receive teaching, and it is up to parents to determine the level and method of engagement with each child. I grew up in a blended family, and I think I would have responded better if kinder forms of correction had been employed.

Competition is rife for our children's attention. They are exposed to a wide array of risks, so there is much they can keep hidden from their parents. If we consistently rebuke them, our attitude will adversely impact their happiness in the home, forcing them to close down and find solace elsewhere.

When I was fourteen years old, I ran away from home and went to a friend's house. I had seen how well her mother treated her. My mother, in contrast, was an extreme disciplinarian who grasped at every opportunity to punish me even when I was not guilty of anything. I felt, therefore, that I could not do anything right. I was broken, had no self-esteem, and if a stranger had appeared and beckoned me, "Come," I would have complied without a second thought. Luckily, it turned out right in the end.

My easy-going stepfather dared not intervene as my mother rained terror on me. I returned home eventually, and my mother's behavior improved noticeably.

Don't fall into the trap of comparing your family to other blended families. Appearances can be deceiving; no one has it all together. Instead, concentrate on your family, let things happen organically, and don't be preoccupied with the sentiments of others.

Communication Issues

Improve your communication skills. If communication within your blended family is poor, you'll feel like you are not in control and lambaste your children even more. Instead, it is best to define boundaries, sustain open communication and build bridges where these are needed. Don't yield to the temptation to yell at or curse at the children. An angry household is not a happy household. When you yell, you teach your children to behave likewise when faced with challenging circumstances. Don't be surprised if they raise their voices in return when you taught them the technique.

Raising children in a blended family can be frustrating and overwhelming. It can test your endurance irrespective of how patient you are. There will be moments when you doubt your ability to hold the family together, and, without intending to, you explode and rain terror on your stepchildren and partner. It can be painful to be unacknowledged or disrespected despite all you do as a stepparent.

Children often test their parents, but you acquire valuable experience and expertise to take you to the next level when you pass the test. True strength lies within, and you'll find it if you consciously reach for it. There will be no growth if everything is easy and there is no challenge.

As parents, we have to dot the I's and cross the T's of others as we punctuate our way through life, adding value to those we care for. When you are entrusted with raising a child with any form of impairment, you embark on a journey that takes you out of your comfort zone and transforms you into a person of value not only to your family but to society. It may not feel like it, but these tests hone your skills for broader impact. The key is believing in the possibilities and the processes necessary to bring them to fruition, even before they can become a reality.

Include the children in decision-making and make them accountable and responsible for distinctive roles within the family unit. If things become overwhelming, take some time with your partner one-on-one and work it out. You are in a partnership and must find time to support each other for the sake of a happy stepfamily. When you adopt a collaborative approach to discipline, you'll reduce your stress levels, the challenges will become easier to overcome, and minor hiccups will have no way of escalating into issues of significant proportion.

And while we're at it, I must mention the need to avoid using swear words in the presence of and for addressing children. Some stepparents find the use of swear words funny and consider it harmless. Some even mentioned that the children understand that they should not repeat curse words. I believe this approach is short-sighted and erroneous. Why would you teach your child lessons that they cannot utilize freely? We may not see them as lessons, but that's exactly what they are.

Offence and Punishment

Irrespective of how unruly your children may be, they do not deserve extreme punishment or abuse. They will never understand or welcome abusive or extreme punitive behavior from their parents or stepparents. No one enjoys constant battering, whether it be verbally or physically. We can destroy our children's ability to experience joy, making them develop hatred for us.

A destroyed self-esteem is of no value to anyone. It creates an excuse for the child to misbehave and disrupt the family unit. Trust breaks down, and love goes out the window. The stepchildren will no longer be your allies and they will grab any opportunity to unseat you. This situation is perilous when a threatening ex-partner is waiting in the wings.

It is said that honesty is the best policy and whether you agree with that sentiment or not, you can at least agree that honesty with oneself is a good policy. That being said, let's acknowledge that sometimes our anger has nothing to do with the child but is due to our frustrations with life. We juggle personal issues with external factors which often make us fearful or anxious. The child's unacceptable behavior is often "the straw that breaks the camel's back." Once we recognize this, and take note for the next time we are angry, we will behave differently, and even if our kindness is taken for weakness we'll be well on our way to having a more peaceful existence.

If you are always bitter and angry, you will put a strain on your family and repel the very people you are trying to love. You will also damage your friendships and other relationships with your own hands, leaving you alone to pick up your pieces.

If you're struggling to connect as a blended family, consider getting professional help. No one is born a stepmom or stepdad; it takes learning and time. You may have unresolved feelings from prior experiences– divorce and separation, death in the family, abuse or neglect. These feelings can come to the fore and overwhelm a family if the parents have not laid them to rest. They inspire negativity, cause conflict, and stir up anger. An honest conversation with an unconnected and objective professional can help your stepfamily heal from issues of the past.

Key points

- Anger can destroy your children's joy, and that will make them develop hatred for you.
- Be the parent that empowers, lifts, and encourages—even if your actions are not reciprocated, your peace of mind depends on it.
- Endeavor to ensure that your actions uplift your children and that these actions are not soul-destroying.

Chapter 3

UNFORGIVENESS

"You don't have to flex your muscles in order to win; learn to drop it, leave it, and let it go"

One of the qualities that destroy us human beings is our inability or unwillingness to forgive. When we hold on to past pain, we hurt ourselves and others. Unforgiveness is a failure to let go and forgive people who have offended you. It is characterized by bitterness, resentment, and animosity and may be accompanied by a hunger for punishment or restitution. This state of affairs causes emotional and mental distress.

Children have parents for a reason. We are there to guide and protect, teach and inspire. Children sometimes make mistakes or break the rules—that's what children do. In their eagerness to explore and make sense of the world, they often venture steps in the wrong direction. We cannot guard against or protect them from every single mistake. Our role is to be there before, during, and after these steps have been taken.

With all the pressures and life challenges we encounter, we cannot afford to hang on to negative baggage. So, for example, don't keep reminding Johnny that he made the same mistake last week and perhaps the week before, and here he is doing it again. In your mind, you think you are saying, "Please stop doing that," while in his mind, he hears, "you are stupid and useless, Johnny."

Setting the Stage

All children misbehave at times; it is called being a child. Your stepchild may react to the change in family life by misbehaving more often than is acceptable. Remember that their whole world has changed, and change is often uncomfortable. They need stability, reassurance and routine—which includes boundaries balanced with love and understanding.

With your partner, think about your expectations for the children, how you can apply consistent rules and boundaries, and how you can help them grow into respectful, responsible adults. At the same time, don't forget that the transition of entering a blended family can be pretty significant for some kids.

Remember why you're in a blended family. You chose your partner, knowing they have children or that you have children with someone else. With that may come some drama left over from former relationships. A partner with kids comes as a package deal, and you'll have to contend with every part of that package—even if there are messy, complicated and stressful parts. Your role is to love and support and thus give your stepfamily the best chance for survival.

Letting Go

Your partner may come into your life with children, parents, ex-partners, friends and extended families, and they may not all accept you. But, if you prioritize finding ways to show love to your partner and your stepchildren, things will fall into place in due course. It is normal to be hurt, but you shouldn't remain wounded. Learn to drop it, leave it and let it go!

When you nurture ill feelings, you hurt yourself in the process. You kill your joy, and the resulting sadness adversely impacts the stepfamily and puts it on a downward spiral. Conversely, when you forgive and let go, you liberate yourself, carving the path to peace and joy in your family unit.

This attitude of holding on to past hurts creates a domino effect that negatively impacts every part of us—our spirit, emotions, thoughts, behaviors, physical body, and relationships. When there is unforgiveness, time stands still and wounds don't heal. Unforgiveness causes wounds to fester; it prolongs the pain. The longer we bear a grudge, the heavier the burden on our spirit becomes. Think of it like this: instead of pulling up and discarding the weeds of pain, we water and nurture them so they become fortified. In time they extract the nutrients from the surrounding support structure, and we are rooted up with it—and just as a giant tree planted near a house grows and damages its foundation, so unforgiveness destabilizes our homes.

Develop strategies to handle issues once and for all and when they recur, correct them without resurrecting past failures. Some of your stepchild's actions will hurt indeed, but you must make an effort to let go, no matter how intensely you have been affected. It may take time to get over it, but time is a great healer. Unforgiveness will hurt the child and lead to physical and mental illness. In addition, it will cause ill feelings in the home and leave open sores that will be hard to heal.

I could not talk about forgiveness without mentioning forgiveness of your former partner if you have had a separation or divorce. You may have to forgive yourself and forgive your ex and his family. Forgiveness does not mean that you condone hurtful actions or that there should be no consequences for such actions. Forgiveness means that you let go of it. You let go of the feeling of wanting revenge for the pain you have suffered. It can take time, and you may have to work at it, but it can and must be done if you want to heal and find happiness.

Changing Faces

There is a saying that holding onto a grudge is like drinking poison and expecting another person to die from it. Unforgiveness creates stress, tension, bitterness, and anger—a deadly combination. Stress can cause physical, physiological, and emotional issues in your body. Juggling the demands of family life is stressful enough; there is no need to add the heaviness of unforgiveness to the mix. It affects your character—pain becomes your identity and steals your joy. Unforgiveness is like a trap, and when you fail to escape, you turn on yourself and others, and you become suspicious and cynical. In addition, research has shown that unforgiveness impairs the body's ability to heal and is a recipe for chronic pain, high blood pressure, a weakened immune system, reduced sleep, and cardiovascular problems.

Don't punish yourself for failures you had in your previous relationships. You can self-harm through actions like self-sabotage, seeking unhealthy coping mechanisms, speaking negatively to yourself, and letting yourself go.

Once you understand that you are not perfect and a work in progress, you will be well on your way to finding happiness. No one has it all together, and mistakes help us grow. If you are struggling to let go of those mistakes and continue to punish yourself, seek help from a counsellor.

Professionals can help you gain perspective and process your past. They can empower you to learn better ways to treat yourself and interact with others. Forgiving yourself will give you the freedom to thrive if you allow yourself to learn the lessons from your past and protect your heart.

Key points

- When you fail to forgive, you hurt yourself in the process, and it is impossible to love others when you struggle to love yourself.
- You have the right to be hurt but not to remain wounded; learn to drop it, leave it, and let it go.

Chapter 4

NEPOTISM

One day we come to realize what's truly important in life. It's not money, the job, or stuff. It's people!

Children are generally resilient, and, despite the occasional bout of jealousy and sibling rivalry, they learn to share and get along with each other in time. Younger children are more likely to welcome a new brother or sister, especially those around the same age.

However, there are instances where children need more time to adapt to the new structure and may not be happy in their stepfamily. In addition, they may be contending with environmental and social pressures, which they may not have disclosed to their parents.

Nepotism rears its ugly head in all types of families. Parents can favor one biological child over another for many reasons, including gender, behavior, personality, and personal interests. Stepparents often favor their biological children over their stepchildren, which can cause various problems, including depression, low self-esteem, and lack of self-confidence later in a child's life.

The Pet Phenomenon

Unfortunately, some stepparents never emotionally connect with their stepchildren and may even treat them with hostility, resentment, and jealousy. If the new couple has a biological child together, often that child becomes the pet, and it is easy for the stepchild to feel isolated and unloved. This can cause long-term problems for the stepchild, who may demonstrate higher levels of aggression and poor performance in school. Some may describe this behavior as attention-seeking, but I do not doubt that there can be genuine hurt on the part of the child. Stepparents must take note of this behavior early and reassure the child.

Fairy tales throughout the ages have unfairly promulgated the concept of "the wicked stepmother", but we also have parents who are unkind to their biological or adopted children in equal measure. When a parent or stepparent overtly or covertly, intentionally or not, treats one of the children in the stepfamily less favorably than another, they are sowing discord in their family. It is like serving poison for dinner.

Parents often have favorites among their children. Sadly I have had first-hand experience of this, and I tell you in no uncertain terms, it was painful. I was the "outside" child, and I felt like an unwanted child! Although my mother was fair in supplying all my physical needs, she wasn't able to make me feel loved. As a result, I had a lot of fear, and my confidence was non-existent. As a result, I know from personal experience that nepotism also occurs unfavorably towards biological children; we mustn't assume it's always the stepchild who is mistreated.

Parents favor children based not only on bloodlines but also for other reasons—a child's perceived intelligence, ability, looks, and skin color. Therefore, biological parents and stepparents must be self-aware and vigilant to ensure they are not guilty of emotional abuse due to personal bias.

In my case, I felt that I was not my mother's biggest fan because I was close to my absent father. I looked forward to those weekends when he would visit, and I enjoyed our days out together. To add insult to injury, I physically resembled my dad and his family, so I was a constant reminder to my mother of her failed relationship with my father.

Your biological children may receive gifts from their grandparents and extended family while your stepchildren look on. There may be times when grandparents wish to take their grandchildren on vacation. Manage these dynamics so the stepchild does not feel left out of the equation. These are some of the external factors that may disrupt the harmony in the stepfamily. Stepparents must expect them to surface and develop strategies to mitigate any visible negative emotions.

I recognize that some things are out of your control, but there is always something you can do. For example, take the stepchild for a special treat when their stepsibling is away. Have a night in with them—watch a movie or play games. Reassure them that they are loved and explain that the grandparent loves them too but could not take them. Children do hurt, but they are more resilient than people think. Once they understand the dynamics, they are unlikely to hold resentment.

While you are developing relationships with your stepchildren, it's important to remember to continue to bond with your biological kids. You do not want to encourage or create an environment of jealousy in the home. Therefore, take care not to neglect your children as you juggle your new family.

Make time to spend with your biological children, whatever their age. Continue with your previous activities, like attending their school's sports day or watching your child perform in a concert. Make time to drop them off at their extracurricular activities and make that time count with interesting conversation. When you regularly give your child your undivided attention, it reminds them that they are important to you, despite all the changes in your home. With a larger family to support, you may work longer hours. Whatever you do, make quality time for your children and stepchildren so that you can have a cohesive, happy home to go to at the end of the day.

Collateral Damage

Parental favoritism can damage relationships between stepsiblings and half-siblings. The siblings might compete for their parents' affection, or they might never really blend. Jealousy may set in, and they might never develop a close relationship. Open communication is an excellent way of addressing this problem. The sooner there is an open and honest dialogue about the feelings and struggles of those involved, the sooner the issue will be resolved.

Stepfamilies with a disabled child in their family unit must be particularly vigilant to ensure that they do not ignore the other children. It may be that they are not showing favoritism to the child with special needs, but they are more attentive to that child for obvious reasons. Other children in the family may feel that their mom or dad is less attentive to them because the disabled child demands so much more of their time. Always make time to reassure the other children and involve them in the care of their stepsiblings.

When you favor one child over another, it hurts the child who is left behind feeling unloved and affects the relationship that this child has with other children in the family. The stepchild might harbor ill feelings towards biological children, which may cause tension between them. Favoritism can be a huge obstacle for a child trying to assimilate into a stepfamily—making bonding almost impossible.

Some parents may not know that the favoritism they show to one child often hurts all the children, including the favorite or the pet, as some may call it. When siblings get on well, they do not want to see their sister or brother, biological or otherwise, being mistreated. It hurts the favored child, who often does not have the power or the courage to protest.

Far too many stepfamilies have experienced extreme and disturbing levels of preferential treatment. Stepparents must understand that all children crave love and attention and once they decide to be a stepparent, they must strive to meet this equitable universal hunger. For this to happen, stepparents must become very aware of the needs of each child and carefully consider how to engage with that child. Without a deliberate attempt to avoid nepotism, it is easy to isolate children and end up with somewhat inadvertent favoritism.

Key points

- When you favor one child over another, it hurts the child who is left feeling unloved and affects the relationship that this child has with other children in the family.
- When siblings get on well, they do not want to see their sister or brother mistreated; it hurts the entire family.

Chapter 5

DEARTH

"A poverty mindset is not inherited; it is cultivated"

Resources of any kind are not infinite. As a result, families find themselves making choices and often deny their children gadgets or other items that their hearts desire. Unfortunately, some parents and stepparents have adopted a scarcity mentality for no justifiable reason.

Many of us grew up in families where funds were genuinely scarce, and our parents had to make tough choices. Those were difficult days, and the skills we learned enabled us to manage our lives in an increasingly commerce-driven world. However, some people have adopted a poverty mindset as a default. They are trapped with the notion that they can hardly afford even the basics. As a result, they deny their children opportunities to pursue extracurricular activities—even when they occur in their local community. As a result, their children miss out on school outings and other events that would be wonderful experiences for them.

Some parents buy the cheapest brand of food available, and eating out is a rarity. They don't take holidays abroad and do not contribute to fundraising or charitable endeavors despite maintaining healthy bank accounts.

The absence of little luxuries and treats has very little to do with the family's disposable income. It is simply down to a deeply ingrained attitude of unaffordability irrespective of their bank balance. Some parents fail to release the shackles of the past, choosing instead to retain behaviors that used to be necessary for survival. And now that there are more resources, they cannot appreciate their improved circumstances. In most cases, the parents may not even be aware of the impact of their actions on their stepfamily.

The situation may become even more toxic if a family isolates itself, fearing the potential financial cost of entertaining people in their homes or attending social events. Consequently, their dearth experience generally goes unnoticed and remains unchallenged.

It is important to note that stepparents who demonstrate this attitude do not set out to hurt their stepchildren and endanger their stepfamilies. This is because, in their minds, they believe that they are taking the best course of action for their family. Some of these families are in custody battles or conflicts with their ex-partners—events that can harm the family's finances. The perception that their financial stability is threatened causes stepparents to keep a tight rein on their finances, securing them as if their lives depend on economic security.

The Scarcity Mindset

A scarcity mindset is the inherent feeling that there will never be enough. This leads to unproductive, unnecessary and self-defeating thoughts. A person with a scarcity mindset believes that opportunities are few and far between, so they must do all they can to hang on to what they have. This could not be further from the truth because new opportunities emerge constantly. When we adopt an abundance mindset, which I will discuss below, we position ourselves to grab these opportunities and capitalize on them.

Kids who grow up in scarcity suffer from the consequences throughout their lives. Child poverty can impact brain development, leading to mood disorders and substance abuse later in life. While stepfamilies with a scarcity mindset may not starve their children of food, they starve them of goods, services, and experiences that can enhance childhood happiness.

There may be, in fact, a positive side to maintaining a scarcity mentality. Parents prioritize their choices and focus on needs rather than wants. Scarcity focuses the mind on particular goals, ensuring that you effectively use what you have. Distractions are less tempting as you try to get more out of every dollar. However, this position must not be at the expense of a happy childhood.

The Concept of Money

Many of the preconceived notions we have about money are established during childhood. In some households, it isn't uncommon to hear parents say: "We don't have that kind of money," or "We can't afford that," even before they hear the price. This mindset can result in fear, anxiety, uncertainty about the future, and stress.

While it is necessary to avoid careless expenditure, it is also essential to have a family life. Your children are part of a wider community, and making them feel excluded augurs badly for a happy future.

Children don't have the maturity or experience to understand a constant sense of lack. Whatever their age, they need you to help them feel comfortable in their family unit. Avoid harping on how much things cost and how your family cannot afford them. That attitude does not inspire confidence and makes them worry about the future. They will become disgruntled if they feel their peers are leaving them behind.

Children must be taught life skills in an intentional and balanced way—including using money wisely and saving for the future. Parents can teach financial skills without denying their children opportunities to enjoy their childhood.

When your children introduce the idea of acquiring something, listen to them without judging or pressuring them to change their minds. Before saying, "We can't afford it", ask yourself, "Is this worth the expense?" That statement opens up the mind about what you can afford. If the item is unnecessary, find ways to teach your children the principles of choice, decision-making, and opportunity cost. Explain that they may have to forgo one thing for another because of financial pressures. But there is no need to live below your means intentionally. That attitude only curtails ambition as it directly courts a scarcity mindset. Instead of closing them down, teach your children to spend their time and energy in creating ways to have the means to access what they want from a mindset of abundance. Use powerful, positive words to empower and ignite an entrepreneurial and resourceful spirit in your children and stepchildren.

Additional Expenses

Families caring for children with special needs and disabilities generally have added expenses. These may consist of transportation costs, specialist equipment, special foods and clothing or the cost of care and therapy. Thankfully, the government has some financial benefits available to families caring for disabled or differently-abled children.

A quick search on the internet reveals various organizations that offer support in the form of grants for specific items or services. To begin, look at the Social Security Benefits for People with Disabilities website for the United States of America—www.ssa.gov/disability, where you can ascertain the various programs you can access for support. If you are in the United Kingdom, you can find information on government support at the website: www.gov.uk/browse/disabilities/benefits.

Whether you have a typical family or a stepfamily, finance is, for the most part, a challenging subject. However, every person incurs costs, and as parents and stepparents, we must do all we can to meet our children's needs and satisfy some of their wants. On the other hand, we shouldn't limit their life chances by curtailing their exposure to experiences that can enrich their lives and widen their knowledge and understanding of the world. It doesn't mean that you must spoil the children. Indeed this is not an either/or scenario. It is about striking the right balance within the scope of available resources to have a healthy family so the children can have great childhood memories.

An Abundance Mindset

The alternative to a scarcity mindset is an abundance mindset. When stepparents embrace an abundance mindset, they position themselves to have more choices and resources in their families. An abundance mindset states that there is plenty available for everyone. Achieving an abundance mindset requires a clear and present mind. It may not be an easy undertaking and will require patience and persistence, but working to shift from a scarcity mindset to one of abundance is worth the effort.

The first steps in developing an abundance mindset are recognizing that you have a scarcity mentality and then deciding that you want to adopt an abundance mindset. To succeed in your endeavor to make this shift, you must start making small sustainable changes in your parenting style and live a little. Please keep an open mind, and, instead of saying an outright "NO" when the stepchildren ask for something, use the opportunity to teach them life skills.

In developing an abundance mindset, you must be flexible and open to new opportunities. A scarcity mindset makes it difficult to embrace change because you focus on challenges rather than on opportunities. An abundance mindset allows you to see things from a different perspective, and you will find better ways of achieving your goals. It does not mean you must exchange your core beliefs for others; you must be true to yourself throughout the process.

An abundance mindset requires a positive attitude; there is less focus on the negative aspects of your life and more on your aspirations. When you have an abundance mentality, you are happy to support others, and you will build relationships with your family members and with people wider afield. Those with a scarcity mentality miss out on this because they usually focus inwards rather than on other people's needs. A healthy balance must be pursued and achieved.

The cultural change from scarcity to abundance in your household is not dependent solely on you. However, it starts with you, so it depends largely on whether you have an abundance mindset in your family unit. What you think will determine if that happens.

Key points

- Don't limit your children's life chances by curtailing their exposure to experiences that can enrich their lives and widen their knowledge and understanding of the world.
- The cultural change from scarcity to abundance in your household is not dependent solely on you, but it does start with you.

Chapter 6

ENNUI

Don't be surprised if people stop listening if you are singing the same song all the time.

Sometimes, parents fall into such a routine that they find it difficult to break the monotony and have fun with their children. Their family runs like a well-oiled machine—very inflexible and highly predictable.

These families do not necessarily have financial issues; the parents may be tired, lethargic, or unmotivated. They think their life is exemplary, but the truth is they are bored, and so are the children. They are doing what needs to be done, but while it seems to be working on the surface, there is no soul in the family unit. The children have come to accept the status quo and turn to each other to find activities to cope with their boredom. They may also spend time online playing games but avoid physical and social interaction with their peers whom they think have more exciting lives. The children make the best of a bad situation and can emerge unscathed but with very few good memories to celebrate. Their self-confidence can also be damaged and take a long time to repair.

Some studies indicate that boredom is appropriate for children as it helps them develop their creativity and boosts their problem-solving skills. While there may be some credence to that, I can see no benefit in maintaining a mundane environment that hosts a boring family life. Your stepchild may be coming from a vibrant family environment where they had lots of choices. Should they find themselves in a joyless space, don't be surprised if they start to rebel.

Strategies for Tackling Boredom

A walk to the nearby park is a good start, but for this family, there is no time for that, or so they think. If mom or dad is ailing, the situation gets worse. The family sinks into a mundane lifestyle with no excitement, no surprises, and no joy. The routine becomes home-school-home. If they are religious, they may go to their place of worship one day per week and attend the occasional birthday party, but they will never be able to host their own party.

While you cannot entertain your children all the time, you must build activities into their lives that will challenge their minds or let them use their hands. These activities may include indoor and outdoor games, visits to places of interest, picnics, or other activities that will break the monotony.

A long list of activities may be possible for your stepfamily, depending on where you live. These include bird-watching, visiting museums, attending performances, playing music, painting, hiking, stamp collecting, among others. With so many choices available, it's difficult not to find something that a stepfamily will enjoy.

One game I like to play with my family is tree-hugging in the forest or the park. It is an exciting game that challenges their minds and improves their memory, imagination, and focus. This is a game played in pairs. One person is blindfolded and led to a random tree by a partner. With the blindfold on, the person is asked to familiarize him or herself with the tree by touching it, hugging it, feeling the roots, bark and other distinguishing features. That person is then led a distance away and the blindfold is removed. The person is then asked to find the particular tree. This game could also be played using items in the home such as a set of different pens. On most occasions, the individual can find the tree or pen successfully, using senses apart from sight.

Thinking creatively is a sure way to beat boredom, but the inability to plan and follow through sometimes gets in the way.

The Beauty of Creativity

Stepparents can banish boredom quickly if they think creatively. If young children become bored with their toys, you might show them how to use them differently. For example, instead of building the same tower repeatedly, ask them to construct a farm by combining other toys. They may even be able to design a zoo. Ask them to consider which animals can cohabit and which ones will be at risk from the other. Let them build little stories in the process. Use craft supplies to decorate the dollhouse and get some new clothes for the doll. Use time at home with your stepchildren to nurture their curiosity.

Join in with your older children to build something worthwhile. For example, you could repurpose items around the house or items accessed from a thrift shop. But no matter how proactive you are, your activities won't fill your child's time for the entire day. Another idea is for them to write stories and draw pictures. They may stumble upon a new passion or hobby that could eventually become a side hustle. These activities build self-esteem and confidence while improving their creativity and entrepreneurship skills.

Children with ADHD and cognitive disabilities may find it harder to occupy themselves for long periods. Their attention spans and focus are usually shorter, so activities quickly lose their novelty and soon enough, they're off to the next activity. This is not the case for all children, though. For example, my daughter has Down syndrome and is happy to remain in one space and play with a single item for hours. Remember that each child is an individual, and you must get to know what your child likes and tailor your response accordingly. Do not copy what another family does; it may not work for your stepfamily.

If you look on the internet, you may be able to find outlets that offer disability-friendly activities and venues for your special child. Some of these venues are open to all the family and may even offer reduced rates for entry or use of space. In some regions, priority lines are available to children with disabilities and their families. From my experience, some airports will have a special line for people with disabilities and their families to make travel more achievable. So if you are keen to find opportunities to have fun, you will find them.

Whatever your situation, you must make time to have fun with your partner and the children. The stepfamily that plays together stays together.

Time for Love

Spend time alone as a couple. If a child needs special care in the family, ask a family member or a care professional for help. Make sure you have a care plan for whoever will care for your special child. Include everything the caregiver needs to know about them: contact details of relevant professionals, medications, special meals, favorite toys, meal times and other peculiarities. It may cost you money, but it's better to pay with money than pay with your peace of mind. When families unite into a blended family, life gets busy, and child-free time is easily neglected.

Set aside time at regular intervals to do something you and your partner enjoy without the children involved. It may be a simple act such as visiting your favorite beauty spot, going to the movies, or eating out. Date nights and time away from the children are suitable for your family as they give you and your partner the chance to reconnect, ease tensions, and make plans. It's an excellent opportunity to discuss family issues and talk about anything. It provides a chance to recharge, refresh, and renew your love for each other and the children in your stepfamily.

A famous saying, "All work and no play makes Jack a dull boy," is pertinent here. My mom may not always have been kind to me, but we could always look forward to a family outing during the school holidays. Families must understand that, even with limitations, they must find ways to have fun and build surprises that engender joy in the family unit.

Key points

- Families must understand that even if there are limitations, they must find ways to have fun and build surprises that inspire joy in the family unit.
- You may have to spend money for the privilege, but it's better to spend money than to sacrifice your peace of mind.

Chapter 7

RETICENCE

"Peace and silence are not synonymous"

Effective communication in the blended family increases trust between family members. Open, transparent, and frequent communication reduces misunderstanding and improves the connection between parents, among siblings, and between parents and stepchildren. Conversely, when there is a breakdown of communication, one of the parties shuts down. This behavior damages the stepfamily and encourages people to harbor grudges.

It is very damaging when a stepparent stonewalls or engages in silent treatment towards a child. Withdrawing interaction or refusing to engage with the child threatens the stepfamily's health. The technique can be used to avoid conflict, but it can also be used to exercise control and inflict punishment. The children experience depression and anxiety, and feel unloved and rejected when it happens. It is manipulative and punishing when you exclude or ignore people or give them the cold shoulder or the silent treatment. In essence, you are inflicting emotional or physical harm—a decision over which you have a choice. My mother often used this technique when she argued with my stepfather. Though it was not targeted at the children in the household, it caused the environment to have an unwelcome heaviness, essentially squeezing the joy out of the home.

When Silence isn't Golden

One of the idioms I learned as a child is, "Silence is golden". My parents used that saying to keep the children quiet during a period when they believed that children were to be seen and not heard. Happily, that era has passed, and now everyone has a voice for the most part.

The silent treatment is often triggered when one partner pressures or overwhelms the other with requests, criticism, or complaints. The receiver then responds with silence and emotional and social distance. Giving the silent treatment is of no benefit to the person who has withdrawn. On the contrary, it shows that the individual is consumed by anger and lacking self-control. This behavior creates a significant imbalance with the child and the stepfamily.

While silence or a pause can be used briefly, with an appropriate explanation such as, "I need a minute," to cool tempers after a heated exchange, it is when silence is used as a deliberate strategy to inflict pain and exercise control that it creates a problem. That strategy is never acceptable and is, in fact, damaging. Stepparents may resort to this for a short period to avoid utterings they may regret later. In this case, it is excusable.

Passive aggression is a real phenomenon. Sarcasm, procrastination, sullenness, sabotage, backhanded compliments, spite, and nit-picking are ways that people express aggression indirectly, sometimes without even realizing it. It is not enough to avoid conflict; it is also important to actively address it as it arises. It is incredibly unhealthy for one party to bottle up feelings of resentment in a family.

Maintaining silence for fear of relationship breakdown or avoiding hurting another person's feelings has the exact opposite effect. Not expressing your feelings hurts the other person because they will know something is wrong and may not even know what it is. When our children display the same behavior it hurts us, so why would it not hurt them when we do it? We all understand the importance of good communication in families, but often we ignore this, holding back as we resort to silence.

Communication Woes

The phenomenon of silence is more prevalent in families where the power dynamics are out of balance and one party feels they have more to lose if they cause the other to be angry.

It does not take much to get overwhelmed by your blended family structure, especially if a custody battle is in progress. Try to comprehend the situation and do your best under the circumstances. Often your anger is not brought about by members of your stepfamily but by people attached to the family—an absent parent or former in-laws. It is easy to go quiet to avoid unleashing your anger onto your stepfamily when this occurs.

If, for example, you find that you are fighting with your ex and this is disturbing your peace, try harder to work things out with the absent parent to reduce your stress level and achieve peace of mind. You may have to make concessions. When you stop seeing your former partner as an enemy and instead try to work with them, it makes things easier for all involved.

I used to be amid conflicts between my parents when my dad visited and wanted to take me out for the day. My mother hated that idea, and she always rebelled. I felt confused when my dad told me to get ready while my mom commanded me to stay put. My dad usually won, but I felt my mother took her revenge on me when I returned home. She often gave me the silent treatment. When she did speak, it was to order me around.

It is necessary to find the right balance between reticence and speaking out. Silence has a place in communication, for in any healthy relationship, parties take turns listening. However, if there are issues to be addressed, prolonged silence is not an appropriate approach to take.

Effective communication is not just about exchanging information. It's about understanding the emotions and intentions behind the information. Not only do you need to convey a message clearly, but you also need to do some active listening to obtain the true meaning of what's being said and be better able to respond in turn. When you learn these skills, you will deepen your connections with your stepfamily and thus build greater trust and respect. This will allow you to work together to improve the well-being of your family.

Words have relevance, but they are not the sole means of communicating with your stepfamily. Your body language and ability to be there for them are equally relevant. Effective communication helps build strong connections between blended family members. Stepfamilies must spend time together and openly address issues that cause conflict. Solid, well-functioning stepfamilies employ various communication methods to interact with one another. They do not resort to silence; instead, they work to build nurturing relationships by treating each other with respect and consideration. They take opportunities to share, whether at the dining table, in the family room, or in their cars. They communicate with their voice and gestures, paying attention to body language and tone of voice as much as they do to the words they choose to use.

Parents must create opportunities for addressing burning issues in an open and non-judgmental atmosphere conducive to listening and learning. When families have fun together, this environment creates opportunities for open communication, and one subject can lead to another. However, if you are seriously aggrieved, try discussing it with your partner first in a calm private space, not when you are angry.

As reticence between the parents is tremendously damaging to relationships, it is in their best interest to avoid it. Failure to do so adversely impacts the relationship satisfaction for both parents reduces feelings of intimacy and reduces the capacity to keep the family in a healthy and wholesome space. Moreover, continued failure to address issues will lead the family into a downward spiral and into an abyss they may never be able to escape.

Key points

- It is not enough to avoid conflict; it is also important to actively address it as it arises.
- Parents owe it to their children to maintain a peaceful environment in their home.
- Resorting to silence is damaging to relationships in the stepfamily.

CONCLUSION

When all is said and done, stepparents are responsible for protecting and caring for the children in their family unit. A man or woman who truly loves their partner will also make every effort to love their stepchildren. Love, however, is a strong word for some people. Nineteenth Century British writer C.S. Lewis once said, "Do not waste time bothering whether you 'love' your neighbor; act as if you did. As soon as we do this we find one of the great secrets. When you are behaving as if you loved someone, you will presently come to love him. If you injure someone you dislike, you will find yourself disliking him more." Sometimes love can be a choice before it is a feeling.

If you find it hard to love your stepchild, the reason may not be because they are not yours biologically; it may just be that your personalities clash or there are other dynamics at play. The child may be misbehaving because they miss their absent parent, blame you for the breakup, or simply have difficulty processing all the changes. When this happens, do not attempt to fight fire with fire. Instead, you must use water to extinguish the fire—don't stoke it or add more fuel by implementing more rules or engaging in a power struggle.

Many of us focus too heavily on the fact that the child is not ours biologically. We tend to forget that biological children also create challenges for their parents. Every parent can recall moments of unhappiness with the behavior of a biological child. I acknowledge that the dynamics change when it's not your child, but sometimes the challenges do not stem from the stepparent relationship. It is simply a child being mischievous as children often are.

Allocate sufficient resources to nurture your stepfamily. Do not deny the children opportunities to engage in extracurricular activities; get in there with them when possible. Adopt an attitude of gratitude and an abundance mindset. Use every chance to teach and inspire your stepchildren to develop life skills and position them for their lives. You will incur additional costs if there is a special child in your family. Conduct research to identify resources available to lessen the impact on your stepfamily.

Only love can conquer hate. Though it requires patience, achieving a happy home is often worth the effort. There is no need to prove anything to a child; be confident in who you are and be the best stepparent possible. Allow your biological children to interact normally with their stepsiblings. Remember, your ultimate goal is to have a happy home. You don't want to live a life filled with drama. Your home should be your safe space; do all you can to preserve it.

Once you are secure in who you are, there is no need to engage in petty fights with children. You are the master of your destiny, and you should not allow anyone to make you fight for what you already know you have or who you are.

Protect your heart by avoiding unnecessary conflict and discord in your home. Entertain neither superiority nor inferiority complex.

Do not expect everyone else to love you, but do love yourself. Low self-esteem can wreck the human spirit and cause you to repel opportunities for love and light. Your future is in your hands. Handle it with care. Embrace your responsibility to raise the next generation—a generation of individuals who will become masters of their destinies.

So there you have it—seven unsuspecting attitudes that are seriously toxic to stepfamilies. Bureaucracy, lambasting, unforgiveness, nepotism, dearth, ennui and reticence are joy killers. They must be kept far from your stepfamily if you expect to achieve that happy, wholesome life you desire and deserve.

Once you have considered and reflected upon your actions concerning the seven elements introduced in this book, let go of any feelings of inadequacy or anger. There is no panacea for building a successful stepfamily, but if you can look in the mirror and honestly say that you have done your best, that is an accomplishment of which you can be proud. Continue to strive for joy in your household—the family that laughs together will stay together. Time is a great healer; make it your ally and be at peace with yourself and others. Treasure each moment, and do not allow the storms of life to blow your house down. Hold on to love and light and know that these too shall pass.

Please Leave a Review

I hope you enjoyed this text.

As an independent author with a small marketing budget, reviews are really important to me. Please remember to leave a review if you bought this book online.

Also, please note that if you purchased the text in a physical store or received the book as a gift, you can still leave a review on Amazon.

Thank you for acquiring this book and thanks on behalf of the families who will benefit from your support.

Other Books You'll Love

The Pocket Learner – Special Needs Education

https://amzn.to/3oyhBIh

The Pocket Learner is an educational system the author initially developed to help her child with special educational needs. The system became an international multi-award-winning innovation and has been extended to families across the globe to help their children build vocabulary, learn to read, and count.

Life Lessons from a Bouncing Ball

https://amzn.to/3AUCH06

This book is a much-needed reminder that play is not just for kids. Apart from stimulating joy and enhancing relaxation, play boosts our creativity and imagination and positively impacts our relationships and personal success. Researchers have found that play isn't just about having fun; it can also be an important means of reducing stress and enhancing our overall well-being.

A GIFT TO OUR READERS

Please join our mailing list to receive periodic updates and materials. You'll also be able to keep abreast of our future publications.

As a thank you please visit the following page or scan the QR code to download a set of original inspirational posters that you can print out, frame and position in your favorite space.

http://eepurl.com/h8SU31

RESOURCES

1. Abraham, K., Studaker-Cordner, M., (n.d.). *Stepchildren Making You Crazy? 5 Ways to Manage Conflict in Blended Families.* Empowering Parents.Com. Retrieved March 16, 2022, from https://www.empoweringparents.com/article/stepchildren-making-you-crazy-5-ways-to-manage-conflict-in-blended-families/

2. *Benefits for People with Disabilities.* (n.d.). Social Security. Retrieved March 15, 2022, fr. https://www.ssa.gov/disability

3. Canda. (2020, June 6). *Forgiveness in Second Marriages.* Blended Restoration. Retrieved March 15, 2022, from http://blendedrestoration.com/forgiveness-in-second-marriages/

4. *Effective communication is the key to blended family success.* (n.d.). Blended and Stepfamily Resource Centre. Retrieved March 16, 2022, from https://blendedfamilyadvice.com/effective-communication -is-the-key-to-blended-family-success/

5. Henry, J. (n.d.). *Family Dynamics.* Https://Irp-Cdn.Multiscreensite.Com. Retrieved March 16, 2022, from https://irp-cdn.multiscreensite.com/6887d51e/files/uploaded/john-henry-psychologist-Family%20Dynamics.pdf

6. Mere Christianity. (n.d.). PBS. Retrieved July 11, 2022, from https://www.pbs.org/wgbh/questionofgod/ownwords/ mere2. html)

7. Miller, G. (n.d.). *The Benefits of Boredom.* The Child Mind Institute. Retrieved March 16, 2022, from

https://childmind.org/article/the-benefits-of-boredom/

8. Rowett, A. (2015, April 14). *The Prison of Unforgiveness*. Bellevue Christian. Retrieved March 16, 2022, from https://bellevuechristiancounseling.com/articles/the-prison-of-unforgiveness

9. Scott, K. (n.d.). *The effects of the silent treatment in families and relationships*. ABC Everyday. Retrieved March 16, 2022, from https://www.abc.net.au/everyday/the-effect-of-silent-treatment-in-relationships-families/11059348

GLOSSARY

PART 1: BLENDED FAMILIES

ASD = alienated stepdaughter
ASS = alienated stepson
BD = Biological dad or biological daughter
BF = Boyfriend
BM = Biological mom
BP = Biological parent
BS = Biological/Birth son
CO = Custody order
CP = Custodial parent
CPS = Child protective services
CS/CSO: Child Support / Child Support Order
DD = Dear/darling/direct daughter
DF = Dear/Darling fiancé/fiancée
DH = Dear/darling husband
DS = Dear/darling son
DW = Dear/darling wife
EOW/EOWE = Every other week/weekend (in custody schedule)
FH = Future husband
FSK(s) = Future step kid(s)
FW = Future wife
GAL = Guardian ad litem
GF = Girlfriend
HC = High conflict
HCBD = High-conflict biological dad
HCBM = High-conflict biological mom
HCP = High-conflict parent/person
MIL/FIL/SIL/BIL = The in-laws
MW = Mini wife
NACHO = Not your kid, not your problem
NCP = Non-custodial parent
OH = Other half
PAS = Parent Alienation Syndrome
PC = Parent coordinator
RO = Restraining order
ROFR = Right of first refusal
SAHSM: Stay at Home Stepmom
SD = Stepdad or stepdaughter
SF = Stepfather
SK = Step kid(s)
SM = Stepmom
SO = Significant other
SS = Stepson
STBX = Soon-to-be ex
TOM = The other mom

PART 2: Special Education

ADA (Americans with Disabilities Act): Provides enforceable guidelines and actions when working with an American with disabilities.

ADD (Attention Deficit Disorder): A child who has this neurobiological disorder may have difficulties with self-control and paying attention and will also exhibit inappropriate behavior at times.

ADHD (Attention Deficit Hyperactivity Disorder): A child with this disorder will have the same problems as one with ADD, but is also hyperactive.

APD (Auditory Processing Disorder): APD affects a child's ability to interpret and understand speech. They may have language delays or difficulty learning in a standard classroom.

APR (Annual Performance Report): An APR covers the student's progress. It is sent to the US Department of Education for monitoring purposes.

ASD (Autism Spectrum Disorder): Previously known as Asperger's Syndrome or autism, ASD is developmental in nature and affects how the child interacts with their environment verbally and non-verbally.

ASL (American Sign Language): ASL is the main sign language used by deaf communities in the United States.

AT (Assistive Technology): AT is technology designed to help people with disabilities perform tasks or increase skills. Examples of AT include wheelchairs, closed captioning, speech-to-text typing, and hearing aids.

AYP (Adequate Yearly Progress): These are standards established by state education departments covering the amount of progress a student should make in a given year.

BD (Behavior Disorder): This acronym covers inappropriate behaviors and difficulties with social interactions that interfere with learning.

BIP (Behavioral Intervention Plan): After observing a student in an educational context, special education educators create a BIP to address specific behavior modifications and goals.

CC (Closed Captioning): CC refers to the text that is added to the bottom of the television screen to duplicate the audio. It is an assistive tool for individuals with hearing loss.

CCSS (Common Core State Standards): These academic standards are established in Math and English literacy to show what a student should accomplish at each grade level.

CD (Cognitive Delay): A child with cognitive delay is performing intellectually below the norm which impacts his or her education.

CP (Cerebral Palsy): A child with CP has difficulty controlling over bodily movement. It is caused by abnormal brain development or injury.

DD (Developmental Disability): A developmental disability occurs when there is a gap between a child's expected level achievement or milestones and their actual abilities at that age.

DS (Down Syndrome): Down syndrome, also known as trisomy 21, is a genetic disorder caused by the presence of a third copy of chromosome 21. Children with Down syndrome often have developmental and learning disabilities.

ED (Emotional Disturbance): An emotionally disturbed child has trouble with learning, social interactions, and exhibiting appropriate behavior.

EI (Early Intervention): EI services are geared to children who show signs of developmental delay at age three or below.

FAS (Fetal Alcohol Syndrome): FAS includes physical and mental defects that develop in a fetus after high levels of alcohol consumption by the mother.

GT (Gifted and Talented): Gifted and talented children have above-average abilities for their age. They require a different approach to education than their peers.

HI (Hearing Impaired): Hearing-impaired means partial or total hearing loss.

IEE (Individual Education Evaluation): An IEE is an independent evaluation of a student's abilities conducted by a non-school employee.

IEP (Individual Education Plan): An IEP lists the goals, timelines, and services that will help a student meet their goals. It is usually developed by a committee of teachers, parents, and other professionals.

LD (Learning Disability): An LD is a disorder of one or more of the psychological processes that are needed to speak, write, listen, do mathematical calculations, and so on.

LRE (Least Restrictive Environment): An LRE is ideal for a student with special needs because it has the most accommodations and the least restrictions to the student's progress.

ODD (Oppositional Defiant Disorder): The ODD child is strong-willed, defiant, and anti-social.

OHI (Other Health Impaired): This covers health problems that affect the child's school performance.

OI (Orthopedic Impairment): An OI describes any orthopedic impairment that impedes a child's education.

PDD (Pervasive Development Disorder): PDD is a diagnostic category that includes socialization and communication disorders. A few disorders under this category are Autism Spectrum Disorder, Rett Syndrome, and Childhood Disintegrative Disorder.

PLEP (Present Level of Educational Performance): As part of an IEP, the PLEP is a statement of the student's current level of functioning and includes their academic strengths, weaknesses, and learning styles.

TBI (Traumatic Brain Injury): Children with a TBI have an injury to the brain that results in mental, physical, or behavioral changes.

VI (Visual Impairment): VI describes a visual impairment that affects educational achievement and school performance.

ABOUT THE AUTHOR

Andrea Campbell, MBA, MA is a social entrepreneur, linguist, and inspirational writer. Since publishing her first business book in 2010, Andrea has released several inspirational books and articles about special needs parenting and personal development, including two Amazon No. 1 bestsellers.

Over the years, she has focused on empowering vulnerable people through education and inspiration. As the mother of a child with special educational needs, she is particularly keen on working with families to enable their disabled children to aspire higher and achieve their potential. She is also the inventor of the Pocket Learner – a set of innovative educational resources for parents, caregivers and educators of children with special educational needs.

Andrea has also published various inspirational coloring books, journals and activity books to empower and inspire people everywhere.

Andrea resides with her family in London, UK, where she continues to positively impact through her writing, creative exploits, training programs, coaching, philanthropy, and inspirational speaking.

www.ingramcontent.com/pod-product-compliance
Lightning Source LLC
Chambersburg PA
CBHW060047230426
43661CB00004B/692